Hometown

Get-Togethers

Also by the editors of *American Profile*

Hometown Recipes for the Holidays

American Profile Hometown Cookbook

Hometown Heroes

Hometown

Get-Togethers

Memorable Meals for Great Gatherings

From the Editors of American*Profile*

Candace Floyd, Anne Gillem,
Nancy S. Hughes, and Jill Melton

wm

WILLIAM MORROW
An Imprint of HarperCollinsPublishers

HOMETOWN GET-TOGETHERS. Copyright © 2008 by Publishing
Group of America, Inc. All rights reserved. Printed in the United
States of America. No part of this book may be used or reproduced
in any manner whatsoever without written permission except in the
case of brief quotations embodied in critical articles and reviews.
For information address HarperCollins Publishers, 10 East 53rd
Street, New York, NY 10022.

HarperCollins books may be purchased for educational, business, or
sales promotional use. For information please write: Special
Markets Department, HarperCollins Publishers, 10 East 53rd Street,
New York, NY 10022.

Photographs by High Cotton Food Styling & Photography

FIRST EDITION

DESIGNED BY NICOLA FERGUSON

Library of Congress Cataloging-in-Publication Data
has been applied for.

ISBN 978-0-06-125790-2

08   09   10   11   12   WBC/QW   10   9   8   7   6   5   4   3   2   1

Contents

Acknowledgments

Without the help of many people, *Hometown Get-Togethers: Memorable Meals for Great Gatherings* would not have been possible.

Our thanks go to *American Profile* magazine's Stephen Duggan, chief financial officer; Charlie Cox, executive editor, and Steve Minucci, director of business development, all of whom cleared the way for this book to be created. Special thanks to Laura Meisner, administrative assistant for Publishing Group of America, who compiled the list of contributors to this book and kept track of the thousands of recipe submissions.

Sarah Durand, our editor at HarperCollins in New York, and her colleagues offered invaluable advice and expertise.

We are grateful to Betty Yandrasits, president of Saint Vincent de Paul Society of Christ the King Catholic Church in Daphne, Alabama, who found recipients for the food prepared in our test kitchen. The elderly, sick, and those who just needed a good meal received the food.

For help in testing the recipes, our thanks go to Robin Brinker, Maura Dismuke, Jessica Hendry, Monica Davis, Maria Skinner, and Libby Allen. For days on end, they helped shop, chop, measure, and clean up, only to start all over again with the next batch of recipes the following day.

Karry Hosford of High Cotton Food Styling & Photography in Natchez, Mississippi, created the beautiful food photography. Our thanks to her as well.

Bringing together these recipes for *Hometown Get-Togethers* was no small task, but it was a rewarding one. Americans' traditions of family and food are alive and well. And all who attend family reunions, church potlucks, and other social gatherings are the fortunate beneficiaries.

Introduction

*P*otlucks, church socials, tailgating parties, and family reunions happen almost every day. And for many home cooks, the first question asked after accepting an invitation is, "What should I bring?"

Social gatherings give home cooks the chance to shine. Fresh seasonal salads, wholesome main dishes, and delectable desserts scaled up to feed a crowd are in order for these events. And to help fill the bill, *American Profile* magazine's readers have once again answered our call for recipes. Just as they did for our *Hometown Recipes for the Holidays,* they sent us nearly 1,500 of their favorite recipes, and here we present more than 170 of the best.

In these pages, you'll find innovative dishes such as breakfast omelets boiled in plastic bags and Reunion Cake and Pie. There are also classics such as Scarborough Fair Herb Bread, using parsley, sage, rosemary, and thyme to make two generously sized loaves; Incredible Chicken Tortilla Soup, which feeds a crowd at church suppers, and Potluck Polynesian Chicken, which garnered not only rave reviews at a community luncheon but also helped facilitate a marriage proposal. The recipes and stories in this book are reminders of the importance of food to family gatherings and community events.

You'll also find the recipes that won prizes in our Hometown Get-Togethers Recipe Contest. Michelle Gauer of Spicer, Minnesota, won the Grand Prize for her Fudge Cappuccino Orange Torte. Blending the rich flavor of chocolate with the sweetness of orange, this dessert is the centerpiece for women's luncheons at Gauer's church and at her own birthday celebrations.

Edgar D. Galbraith of Jacksonville, North Carolina, won the First Place prize for his Taco

Casserole. Galbraith serves this spicy crowd-pleaser at church gatherings and at the awards dinner for his bowling league.

Our final contest winner, in the French's Original French Fried Onions category, was Kathryn Novak of Northville, Michigan. She brings out her recipe for Nona's Italian Country Chicken every Christmas Eve, much to the delight of her large family. She says that her twenty-seven nieces and nephews all love it. We hope you will, too.

Breakfasts

*T*here is nothing better than gathering around the table in the morning with family or friends to share good food and conversation. The occasion might be a weekend at the lake, a visit from hungry grandchildren, a college reunion, or even a stopover during a dogsled race.

Louise Thureen of Two Harbors, Minnesota, had three good reasons to develop her Grandma's Overnight Breakfast Bars—her grandchildren. When her son, daughter-in-law, and their three children arrive, the bars are sure to be waiting. Thureen says coming up with the popular dish has been a mixed blessing—the children love the bars, but she has to make them every time they are coming to visit. Her answer? She's now teaching the kids how to prepare them.

Thureen also spends time each year as a volunteer hostess and cook for the annual John Beargrease Sled Dog Marathon in northeast Minnesota, which has been held for more than a quarter-century. She keeps the racers, volunteers, and officials well fed at the Sawbill Landing Checkpoint, a mandatory stopover. Her South-of-the-Border Breakfast Bake has been a popular dish with the racers.

Jay Bertaccini of Old Forge, Pennsylvania, helped solve a dilemma at a college sorority reunion. Some twenty members of Theta Phi Alpha from Penn State University were due at one of the member's homes for Sunday brunch. The hostess worried about how to have breakfast ready for all simultaneously. Bertaccini came up with Omelet in a Bag for a Crowd—an ingenious way to feed everyone at once and a real conversation piece, too.

Robbie Morgan of Myrtle Point, Oregon, wanted to welcome her new neighbors by hosting a brunch in their honor but was equally concerned about serving healthy fare. She came up with Low-Fat Breakfast Sausage, which starts with lean pork tenderloin. The dish was a hit—and Morgan says she shared the recipe with her new friends.

Carol Ann McClelland of Somers, Connecticut, worked at a bed-and-breakfast inn during the summer months, where one of the most popular breakfast offerings was Fresh Strawberry French Toast. Lucky guests who visit her home now enjoy this seasonal treat. It's a hostess-friendly dish as well, since it can be prepared ahead.

Elda Baumgartner of Rossiter, Pennsylvania, took a sleepy morning mishap and turned it into a popular staple at her breakfast table. She accidentally poured her orange juice into the French toast batter but decided to give it a try instead of starting over. The results were excellent.

Grandma's Overnight Breakfast Bars

Louise Thureen, Two Harbors, Minnesota

Serves 18

"With a son, daughter-in-law, and three grandchildren coming to spend the night with us, I was looking for a breakfast recipe that could be prepared ahead of time, would not take too long to cook in the morning, and would provide a nice tasty hot meal that everyone would like. I cobbled one together that became my grandchildren's all-time favorite. Its success has been a mixed blessing. Every time the grandchildren come for a visit, they want me to make this recipe. I have now been showing them how to make it, as well."

1. Grease a 13×9-inch baking dish.

2. To prepare the bars, combine the flour, oats, flax meal, baking powder, baking soda, salt, and cinnamon in a medium bowl; set aside.

3. Combine the granulated sugar, brown sugar, and butter in a large bowl. Beat with a mixer at low speed until just blended. Increase the speed to high and cream well. Blend in the eggs and buttermilk. Decrease the speed to low and gradually add the flour mixture from step 2, beating until just blended and scraping the sides of the bowl. Fold in the apples. Pour into the prepared pan.

4. To prepare the topping, combine the walnuts, brown sugar, and ground cinnamon in a small bowl; mix well. Sprinkle evenly over the batter. Cover with plastic wrap and refrigerate overnight.

BARS

1¼ cups all-purpose flour

1½ cups old-fashioned oats

2 tablespoons flax meal

1 teaspoon baking powder

1 tablespoon baking soda

¼ teaspoon salt

2 teaspoons ground cinnamon

1 cup granulated sugar

½ cup packed light brown sugar

⅔ cup (10⅔ tablespoons) butter, softened

2 eggs

1⅓ cups buttermilk

2 medium apples, peeled, cored, and chopped

continued

1 cup chopped walnuts or pecans

½ cup packed light brown sugar

1 teaspoon ground cinnamon

5. Preheat the oven to 350°F. Uncover the pan and let stand for 30 minutes. Bake for 45 minutes, or until a wooden pick inserted in the center comes out clean. Serve warm.

TIPS FROM OUR TEST KITCHEN: Flax meal is available at major supermarkets and in health food stores. Substitute 1 cup shredded carrots for 1 apple, if desired. Substitute plain yogurt for the buttermilk, if desired.

Omelet in a Bag for a Crowd

Albert and Julia (Jay) Bertaccini, Old Forge, Pennsylvania

Variable servings

"*M*y wife, Jay, attended a reunion of her sorority, Theta Phi Alpha, from Penn State University. The Sunday brunch hostess was concerned about having food ready for the twenty attendees at the same time, so my wife suggested this recipe. The brunch was a huge success. The attendees enjoyed selecting their own ingredients, and everyone was served together."

1. Fill a stockpot half full of water and bring to a boil over high heat. Have each guest write his or her name on a zip-top bag using a permanent marker.

2. Place the desired vegetables, meats, cheese, and seasonings in each bag. Break 2 eggs on top of the ingredients. Close the bag and squeeze to mix the ingredients. The bags should be about one-third full. Open the bag slightly to release some of the air and seal securely. Place a few of the bags into the boiling water.

3. Boil for 7 to 20 minutes, depending on the number of bags in the pot. Cooking time will vary. Open the bags to test for doneness. Reseal and return to the pot for a few minutes if not thoroughly cooked.

4. To serve, open the bag and slide the omelet onto a plate.

Quart-size plastic zip-top bags

Chopped onions, broccoli, bell peppers, chiles, shallots, garlic, zucchini, and tomatoes

Ham, cooked bacon or bacon bits, sausage, crabmeat, lobster, and leftover beef and pork

Cheddar, mozzarella, Parmesan, Pepper Jack, Swiss cheese, Asiago, Colby, and Brie

Fresh chives, parsley, sage, thyme, basil, seasoned salt, Cajun seasoning, and black pepper

Eggs (2 per omelet)

TIPS FROM OUR TEST KITCHEN: Use a variety of ingredients to make this dish as simple or elaborate as you wish. Egg whites can be substituted for whole eggs. These omelets are casual and fun—great for a campout or any breakfast get-together.

Petite Quiches

Christina Lowe, Whittier, California

Serves 12

"When our church recently started up a women's ministry, our first get-together was a potluck brunch. I brought my usual orange teacake and some purchased frozen mini-quiches. They were terrible! I was so frustrated I decided to come up with my own recipe. To our next meeting, I brought these quiches, and everybody loved them."

One 17-ounce package frozen puff pastry sheets

Three 6-ounce packages baby spinach leaves

1½ cups shredded Swiss cheese

¼ cup finely chopped no-water-added ham, smoked pork, or cooked bacon

4 eggs

1 large shallot, minced

¼ cup mayonnaise

1 tablespoon Dijon mustard or Trader Joe's Aioli Garlic Mustard

¼ teaspoon black pepper, or to taste

½ teaspoon salt, optional

2 tablespoons olive oil

TIPS FROM OUR TEST KITCHEN: Water-added ham will make the quiches soggy. If no-water-added ham is unavailable, fry bacon until it is soft and then mince it. Do not use bacon bits.

1. Preheat the oven to 400°F. Thaw the puff pastry sheets according to the package directions.

2. Heat a Dutch oven over medium-high heat. Add ¼ cup water and the spinach. Cook for 2 minutes, stirring and tossing gently. Do not overcook. Drain in a colander and press with the back of a spoon to squeeze out excess water. Place on a cutting board and chop finely.

3. Combine the spinach, Swiss cheese, ham, eggs, shallot, mayonnaise, mustard, pepper, and salt, if using, in a large bowl; mix well.

4. Grease two mini-muffin pans using a napkin dipped in olive oil. Unfold the puff pastry sheets. Cut each sheet lengthwise into 3 strips and then cut each strip into 4 pieces. Carefully push each piece firmly into the bottom of a muffin cup. The pastry will fit snugly and overlap a bit.

5. Spoon 2 tablespoons of the spinach mixture into each cup. Bake for 24 minutes, or until the bottoms are golden brown and the edges puff. Rotate the pans halfway through the cooking time if needed for even browning. Serve warm.

Cajun Crab Brunch Bake

Trisha Kruse, Eagle, Idaho

Serves 6

"*T*his dish really captures the flavor of New Orleans. The sautéed 'trinity' of celery, peppers, and onions complements the crab perfectly. The Cajun seasonings give it a nice zip, and the croissants and half-and-half ensure that this dish has the rich, indulgent character of the French Quarter."

1. Preheat the oven to 350°F. Grease an 11×7-inch baking pan.

2. Melt the butter in a medium skillet over medium-high heat. Add the onion, bell pepper, and celery and cook until the vegetables are tender, about 8 minutes, stirring frequently. Remove from the heat and cool slightly.

3. Combine the eggs, half-and-half, crabmeat, croissants, Swiss cheese, Cajun seasoning, and salt in a large bowl; mix gently.

4. Stir the onion mixture into the egg mixture and pour into the prepared pan. Bake for 45 to 50 minutes, until golden brown and set in the center. Let stand for 10 minutes on a cooling rack before serving.

2 tablespoons butter

1 medium onion, finely chopped

1 medium red bell pepper, finely chopped

1 medium celery stalk, finely chopped

6 eggs, beaten

2 cups half-and-half

1 pound fresh crabmeat, picked over for shells and cartilage

8 day-old croissants, torn into 1-inch pieces

1½ cups shredded Swiss cheese

2 teaspoons Cajun seasoning

½ teaspoon salt

Champagne Brunch Casserole

Ashley Murphy, Hastings, Nebraska

Serves 10 to 12

"I make this for weekends at the lake, holiday brunches, and for special treats at work. I keep the recipe on my computer, as I am always asked for a copy!"

SAUCE

3 tablespoons butter

4 green onions, chopped (white and green parts)

1 garlic clove, minced

1 tablespoon all-purpose flour

1½ cups chicken broth

¾ cup Champagne or white wine

⅛ teaspoon ground nutmeg

⅛ teaspoon dry mustard

¼ teaspoon black pepper

½ cup sour cream

10 eggs, beaten

FILLING

5 cups cubed day-old French bread

¼ cup (½ stick) butter, melted

2 cups shredded Swiss cheese

12 ounces ham, cut into ¼- to ½-inch cubes

1. To prepare the sauce, melt the butter in a medium skillet over medium heat. Add the green onions and garlic and cook for 1 minute, stirring constantly. Add the flour; mix well. Stir in the broth, Champagne, nutmeg, mustard, and pepper.

2. Bring to a boil, reduce the heat, and simmer until slightly thickened, about 15 minutes, stirring frequently. Remove from the heat and whisk in the sour cream.

3. Place the eggs in a medium bowl. Add a small amount of the hot mixture to the eggs. Beat the egg mixture into the sauce; blend well.

4. To prepare the filling, grease a 13×9-inch dish. Arrange the bread cubes in the bottom of the prepared pan. Pour the melted butter over the bread cubes and top with the cheese and ham. Pour the egg mixture evenly over the top. Cover the casserole with plastic wrap and refrigerate overnight.

5. Preheat the oven to 350°F. Uncover the casserole and place on a foil-lined baking sheet. Bake for 55 minutes, or until a knife inserted in the center comes out clean.

Huevos Rancheros Casserole

Shirley Wieberg, Penn Valley, California

Serves 10 to 12

"I've shared this recipe with rave reviews at Sunday brunches, church gatherings, Christmas morning family brunches, and family reunions. I serve it with bacon or pork sausage and fruit."

1. Preheat the oven to 325°F. Grease a 3-quart casserole dish or a 13×9-inch baking dish.

2. To prepare the casserole, sprinkle the Monterey Jack in the bottom of the prepared dish. Spoon the chiles evenly over the cheese and top with the Cheddar.

3. Combine the eggs, sour cream, chili powder, and salt in a large bowl; whisk until foamy. Pour over the cheese mixture. Bake, uncovered, for 50 minutes, or until a knife inserted in the center comes out clean.

4. To prepare the sauce, heat the salsa, tomato sauce, and bouillon granules in a small saucepan over medium-high heat until thoroughly heated. Serve the sauce along with the casserole or spoon some sauce onto a plate and top with a serving of the casserole.

CASSEROLE

2 cups shredded Monterey Jack

Two 4-ounce cans chopped green chiles, undrained

1 cup shredded sharp Cheddar

12 eggs

2 cups sour cream

½ teaspoon chili powder

1 teaspoon salt

SAUCE

1 cup salsa

One 8-ounce can tomato sauce

1 teaspoon chicken bouillon granules

Italian Brunch Casserole

Carol Ann McClelland, Somers, Connecticut

Serves 10 to 12

"*M*y mother's late friend Rosie was the best Italian cook I ever knew. She often made this dish when we were invited for Sunday night supper. It was heavenly with her homemade breads, followed by ricotta cheese pie with strawberries for dessert. She shared this recipe with us many years ago, and I've made it often."

1½ pounds mild or hot Italian sausage,
  casings removed

3 tablespoons olive oil

½ large green bell pepper, finely
  chopped

1 medium onion, finely chopped

¾ cup sliced fresh mushrooms

2 garlic cloves, minced, optional

One 28-ounce can diced tomatoes with
  basil, drained

3 cups shredded mozzarella or Italian
  cheese blend

8 eggs

2 cups half-and-half

1 teaspoon dried oregano or dried
  Italian seasoning

½ teaspoon salt

1. Preheat the oven to 350°F. Grease a 13×9-inch baking dish.

2. Crumble the sausage and place it in a large skillet over medium-high heat. Cook until no longer pink, stirring constantly. Drain on paper towels and set aside.

3. Add the olive oil to the same skillet and reduce the heat to medium. Add the bell pepper and onion and cook until the onion is translucent, about 4 minutes, stirring frequently. Add the mushrooms and garlic and cook until the mushrooms are tender, 2 to 3 minutes. Remove the skillet from the heat, and stir in the reserved sausage; mix well.

4. Spread the sausage and vegetable mixture in the prepared pan. Sprinkle evenly with the tomatoes and top with 2 cups of the shredded mozzarella.

5. Combine the eggs, half-and-half, oregano, salt, and pepper in a medium bowl. Whisk until well blended and pour evenly over the top of the casserole. Cover with foil and bake for 40 to 45 minutes, until the edges are set but the center is just slightly soft.

6. Remove from the oven and sprinkle with the remaining cheese and top with the bread crumbs. Bake, uncovered, for 5 minutes longer. Let stand for 20 minutes before cutting into squares to serve.

¼ teaspoon black pepper

1 cup dry Italian seasoned bread crumbs

TIPS FROM OUR TEST KITCHEN: Allowing the mixture to stand the suggested time is a very important step that should not be skipped. It allows the flavors to blend. The same amount of cooked, crumbled bacon or diced, cooked chicken may be substituted for part of the sausage. A smoky ham or smoked sausage may be substituted for the entire amount of sausage. A variety of bell peppers or mushrooms may be used.

Low-Fat Breakfast Sausage

Robbie Morgan, Myrtle Point, Oregon

"I created this breakfast side dish for a brunch to which I invited my new neighbors. I wanted to make changes for a healthier diet, but still wanted to include meat. It was a big hit, and I shared the recipe with them. The sausage tastes great!"

One 1-pound pork tenderloin

½ large red bell pepper, finely chopped

4 green onions, finely chopped (white and green parts)

1½ teaspoons dried red pepper flakes, or to taste

1 teaspoon ground cumin

½ teaspoon salt

¼ teaspoon black pepper

4 teaspoons olive oil

1. Place the steel blade in a food processor and add the pork tenderloin. Process to the consistency of ground sausage.

2. Combine the ground pork, bell pepper, green onions, red pepper flakes, cumin, salt, black pepper, and 2 teaspoons of the olive oil in a medium bowl; mix well. Shape the mixture into 8 patties.

3. Heat the remaining 2 teaspoons olive oil in a large nonstick skillet over medium heat. Tilt the skillet to lightly coat the bottom of the pan. Add the patties and cook until no longer pink in the center, 10 to 12 minutes, turning frequently.

TIPS FROM OUR TEST KITCHEN: Layer leftover uncooked patties between sheets of wax paper and freeze in a zip-top plastic bag.

South-of-the-Border Breakfast Bake

Louise Thureen, Two Harbors, Minnesota

Serves 10 to 12

"As a volunteer hostess and cook for the John Beargrease Sled Dog Race in northeast Minnesota, I help keep the mushers, volunteers, and officials fed for three days each winter. The Sawbill Landing Checkpoint, high in the hills on the north shore of Lake Superior, is a mandatory layover place. I will have hot food, coffee, and cocoa ready, no matter what time they arrive. This recipe is especially easy."

1. Preheat the oven to 350°F. Butter a 13×9-inch baking dish.

2. Bring 6 cups water to a boil in a large saucepan over high heat. Add the potatoes and return to a boil. Reduce the heat and simmer, uncovered, until just tender, about 8 minutes. Drain well and set aside.

3. Heat a large skillet over medium-high heat. Add the sausage and cook until lightly browned, stirring frequently. Add the bell pepper and chiles and cook for 2 minutes. Remove the mixture from the skillet and drain on paper towels. Return the sausage and vegetables to the skillet. Add the potatoes and 1 cup of the French fried onions. Season with salt and pepper. Stir gently to thoroughly blend.

4. Pour the sausage mixture into the prepared pan. Pour the eggs on top, stirring lightly with a fork. Top with the Cheddar and remaining French fried onions. Bake for 30 minutes, or until the eggs are set in the center. Remove from the oven and let stand for 15 minutes to allow the flavors to blend. Serve warm.

Butter

4 medium red potatoes, quartered and cut into ¼-inch slices

1 pound chorizo sausage, casings removed

1 medium red bell pepper, finely chopped

One 4-ounce can chopped mild green chiles, drained

One 6-ounce can French's Original French Fried Onions

Salt and pepper

10 eggs, beaten

1½ cups shredded Cheddar

Fresh Strawberry French Toast

Carol Ann McClelland, Somers, Connecticut

Serves 10 to 12

"I worked at a bed-and-breakfast inn for a few summers. This was one of the most requested favorites on our breakfast buffet. It's convenient, as most of the prep work is done the night before."

3 tablespoons vegetable oil

16 slices day-old sandwich bread, white or light wheat, crusts removed, if desired

One 8-ounce package cream cheese, softened

½ cup sugar

½ cup coarsely ground pecans, optional

8 eggs

2 cups half-and-half

3 tablespoons butter, melted

½ teaspoon ground cinnamon

1 cup strawberry jam or preserves

1 quart ripe strawberries, sliced

1. Pour the vegetable oil into a 13×9-inch pan, tilting to coat the bottom. Arrange 8 slices of the bread in a single layer in the pan, trimming to fit as needed.

2. Combine the cream cheese and ¼ cup of the sugar in a medium bowl; beat until smooth. Stir in the pecans, if using. Spread the mixture evenly over the bread. Top with the remaining bread slices.

3. Mix the eggs and half-and-half in a bowl and blend well. Pour evenly over the bread. Cover tightly with plastic wrap and refrigerate at least 4 hours or overnight.

4. Remove the pan from the refrigerator 30 minutes before baking. Preheat the oven to 375°F. Remove the plastic wrap.

5. Drizzle the melted butter over the top of the egg mixture.

6. Combine the remaining ¼ cup sugar and the cinnamon in a small bowl and sprinkle evenly over the top. Cover the pan with foil and bake for 45 minutes. Remove the foil and bake, uncovered, for 15 to 20 minutes longer, until puffy and golden brown on the sides. Let stand for about 15 minutes before cutting.

7. Heat the jam in a large saucepan over low heat until melted. Remove from the heat and stir in the strawberries. Serve the berry mixture warm on the side.

TIPS FROM OUR TEST KITCHEN: This also works well with fresh blueberries and blueberry jam. For a large crowd, make both kinds of sauces, keeping them on the warming tray so guests can choose what they prefer. Have some maple syrup available, too, and pass whipped topping, if desired.

Orange Juice French Toast

Elda Baumgartner, Rossiter, Pennsylvania

Serves 6 to 12

"One sleepy morning, I accidentally poured my orange juice into the French toast batter. Instead of throwing the mixture away, I decided to use it. Boy, was it good!"

ORANGE SYRUP

2 cups orange juice
2 cups light corn syrup
1 cup packed light brown sugar
½ cup (1 stick) butter or margarine

FRENCH TOAST

1½ cups milk
1 cup orange juice
1 tablespoon sugar
1 tablespoon vanilla extract
1 teaspoon ground cinnamon
⅛ teaspoon salt
3 eggs, well beaten
6 tablespoons butter or margarine
Twelve 1-inch slices white or French bread

1. To prepare the syrup, combine the orange juice, corn syrup, brown sugar, and butter in a medium saucepan. Bring the mixture to a boil over medium-high heat, stirring frequently. Reduce the heat to low and keep warm.

2. To prepare the French toast, combine the milk, orange juice, sugar, vanilla, cinnamon, salt, and eggs in a bowl. Whisk until well blended.

3. Melt 2 tablespoons of the butter in a large non-stick skillet over medium heat. Working in batches, quickly dip 3 bread slices in the egg mixture and place in the skillet. Cook until brown on both sides, 8 to 10 minutes, turning occasionally. Place on a serving platter and cover to keep warm. Continue until all of the bread is cooked, adding additional butter as needed to prevent sticking.

4. Serve with the warm syrup. Refrigerate leftover syrup to serve with waffles, pancakes, or French toast.

Dream Coffee Cake

Laverne Koivisto, Ashtabula, Ohio

Serves 16 to 18

"I take this cake to VFW meetings and our church fish fries. It goes every time, with no leftovers! Try it—it's wonderful."

1. Preheat the oven to 350°F. Grease a 13×9-inch baking pan.

2. Combine the cake mix, vegetable oil, eggs, and sour cream in a large bowl. Beat for 2 minutes with a mixer at low speed, scraping the sides of the bowl frequently. Mix the sugar, cinnamon, and walnuts in a medium bowl.

3. Spread half of the batter in the prepared pan. Sprinkle half of the cinnamon mixture over the top. Repeat with the remaining batter and cinnamon mixture.

4. Bake for 40 minutes, or until a wooden pick inserted in the center comes out clean.

One 18-ounce package yellow cake mix

1 cup vegetable oil

4 eggs

1 cup sour cream

¾ cup sugar

1½ teaspoons ground cinnamon

1¾ cups chopped walnuts

TIPS FROM OUR TEST KITCHEN: This coffee cake tastes of homemade comfort, but it only takes a few minutes to prepare. That's why it's a dream! It may be frozen.

Appetizers

When it's time for family and friends to gather, appetizers are the opening act, setting the stage for the occasion—be it a family dinner, holiday celebration, neighborhood picnic, or an office party. Whether they are casual and fun or elegant palate-tempters, the first course starts things off on the right foot.

Betty Key, of Gardendale, Alabama, always sent her Cheese Ring with Strawberry Preserves when her husband needed to take a dish to an office celebration at the Chevrolet dealership where he worked in Birmingham. It was so popular she usually doubled the recipe—and even after he retired, the employees would call and ask her to make it for them.

A get-together provides the perfect opportunity for Pamela Shank, of Parkersburg, West Virginia, to try out a new dish. Seafood Cheesecake Appetizer is a recent addition to her recipe file and has gotten good reviews. Her large family often spends time together, and she says she likes to have a sophisticated dish to serve.

Carol Snyder, of Sumner, Iowa, wanted to find just the perfect starter for her fiftieth anniversary celebration. After trying several other recipes, she found Gourmet Pecans were the perfect choice. The delicious pecans also make their way into care packages she sends to her college-aged grandsons.

Diane McCrory's fiery Buffalo Wings are a must at family reunions. The Trinity, Texas, cook says they not only are easy to prepare but go well with any entrée—steak, poultry, or fish. And they definitely add spice to the reunions—McCrory says they are "atomic."

JoAnn Geary, of Whispering Pines, North Carolina, thought her Spicy Island Shrimp would be a good choice to take to a friend's Christmas party. But she had to pair detective skills with her cooking skills to solve a party-time mystery. The first time she brought a bowl of the tasty shrimp, it disappeared from the serving table shortly after she arrived. The next year, her shrimp never made it to the buffet table. When Geary asked her friend about the vanishing shrimp, he said he enjoyed it so much that he had decided to keep it for himself rather than share it with his guests. From then on, Geary has given him his own portion as a gift each year.

Brie and Blue Wheel with Macadamia Nuts

Lillian Julow, Gainesville, Florida

Serves 18 to 22

1. Cut the Brie in half horizontally. Remove the top half of the wheel and place the bottom on a large serving platter or cake stand.

2. Combine the Roquefort, sour cream, macadamia nuts, parsley, chives, and pepper in a medium bowl; mix well. Spread evenly over the bottom half of the Brie. Replace the top half of the wheel.

3. Wrap the wheel tightly in plastic wrap and refrigerate for at least 2 and up to 24 hours.

4. To serve, remove the wheel from the refrigerator. While the Brie is still very cold, cut straight down through the layers around the circumference of the wheel in a 1½-inch-wide strip so that you make a ring. Cut the ring crosswise into small pieces, about ¾ inch wide, and set the pieces aside. Cut another 1½-inch-wide strip around the circumference. Place the remaining center section in the center of a platter and arrange the pieces around it in concentric circles.

5. Let stand for 2 hours to bring to room temperature for peak flavors and texture. Serve with breads and crackers.

One 2½-pound wheel of Brie, well chilled

3 ounces Roquefort or other blue cheese, softened

3 tablespoons sour cream

2 tablespoons finely chopped macadamia nuts or cashews, toasted

2 tablespoons finely chopped flat-leaf parsley

1 tablespoon finely chopped chives or green onions (green part only)

½ teaspoon black pepper

Assorted breads

Unsalted crackers

TIPS FROM OUR TEST KITCHEN: The Brie must be well chilled to make it firm enough to slice.

Mini Cheese Balls

Malanna Merriman, Oakland City, Indiana

Serves 15

"I had two Christmas parties in December, and these Mini Cheese Balls were really good—and they were so easy to make."

One 8-ounce container whipped cream cheese with chives and onions, softened

2 cups shredded mozzarella

One 2-ounce jar real bacon pieces

½ teaspoon dried Italian seasoning

1 green onion, chopped (green part only)

¾ cup finely chopped pecans, toasted

1. Mix the cream cheese and mozzarella in a bowl with a mixer until well blended. Add the bacon pieces, Italian seasoning, and green onion.

2. Place the pecans in a small bowl. Shape the cheese mixture into small balls, about 1 level tablespoon each. Roll each ball in the pecans and place on a baking sheet in a single layer. Cover with plastic wrap and refrigerate for 2 hours before serving.

TIPS FROM OUR TEST KITCHEN: If the balls are difficult to shape, place the cheese mixture in the freezer for 30 minutes.

Cheese Ring with Strawberry Preserves

Betty Key, Gardendale, Alabama

Serves 18 to 20

"My husband worked at a Chevrolet dealership in Birmingham, Alabama, for many years. The employees there loved this cheese ring and expected it for every occasion. Even after my husband retired, they called to ask if I would make it for them. I always sent two, and they were gone in no time."

1. Combine the Cheddar, cream cheese, mayonnaise, pecan chips, onion, garlic, and Tabasco in a large bowl; mix well. Cover the bowl with plastic wrap and refrigerate for 2 hours to overnight.

2. Remove the mixture from the refrigerator and shape into a ring on a serving plate. Fill the center of the ring with the preserves. Serve with assorted crackers.

1 pound sharp Cheddar, finely shredded

One 8-ounce package cream cheese, softened

½ cup mayonnaise

1 cup pecan chips, toasted, if desired

1 medium onion, finely chopped

1 garlic clove, minced

2 to 3 tablespoons Tabasco sauce

2 cups strawberry preserves

Assorted crackers

TIPS FROM OUR TEST KITCHEN: If pecan chips are unavailable, finely chop pecan pieces. This recipe can also be shaped into a cheese ball, omitting the preserves.

Goat Cheese Torte

June Laughlin, Lady Lake, Florida

Serves 12 to 16

"Whenever I serve this, it is a big hit. If there is any left over, I freeze it or serve it over hot pasta."

1 pound goat cheese, softened
1 cup (2 sticks) butter, softened
8 ounces jarred basil pesto
½ cup slivered almonds, lightly toasted,
**   if desired**
8 ounces jarred sun-dried tomato pesto
Assorted crackers

1. Cream the goat cheese and butter with a mixer at medium speed until very smooth. Spray a 6-inch springform pan with nonstick cooking spray.

2. Layer one-quarter of the goat cheese mixture, half of the jarred basil pesto, and 2 to 3 tablespoons of the almonds in the prepared pan. Add one-quarter of the goat cheese mixture and half of the jarred sun-dried tomato pesto. For the third layer, add one-quarter of the goat cheese mixture, the remaining basil pesto, and 2 to 3 tablespoons of the almonds. Top with the remaining goat cheese mixture, tomato pesto, and almonds.

3. Cover the springform pan with plastic wrap and refrigerate overnight. Unmold the torte onto a serving plate and let stand for 1 hour before serving. Serve with crackers.

TIPS FROM OUR TEST KITCHEN: It is important to let the torte stand at room temperature before serving for peak flavor and texture. Goat cheese, also known as chèvre, is often sold in 4-ounce packages in the deli case.

Seafood Cheesecake Appetizer

Pamela Shank, Parkersburg, West Virginia

Serves 24

"This recipe has received good comments from everyone. We have a very large family and have many get-togethers. I like to try new things and make dishes that look elegant for special occasions."

1. Preheat the oven to 350°F. Lightly coat a 9-inch springform pan with nonstick cooking spray.

2. Combine the cracker crumbs and butter in a medium bowl; mix well. Press into the bottom of the prepared pan. Bake for 10 minutes.

3. Beat the cream cheese and ¾ cup of the sour cream in a bowl with a mixer until smooth. Add the eggs, lemon juice, salt, and pepper; beat until smooth. Stir in the crabmeat and the white part of the green onions. Spoon into the baked crust.

4. Bake on a foil-lined baking sheet for 45 to 50 minutes, until the top is lightly browned and the center is set. Cool for 20 minutes on a wire rack. Loosen the sides of the pan, but do not remove until completely cooled.

5. Place the torte on a plate, cover with plastic wrap, and refrigerate until serving time. Remove the plastic wrap, spread the remaining ¼ cup of the sour cream on top, and garnish with the green part of the onions. Serve with assorted crackers or party breads.

One sleeve butter crackers, crushed
½ cup (1 stick) butter, melted
Two 8-ounce packages cream cheese, softened
1 cup sour cream
3 eggs
1 teaspoon lemon juice
½ teaspoon salt
⅛ teaspoon black pepper
8 ounces cooked fresh crabmeat or chopped cooked shrimp
4 green onions, chopped (keep white and green parts separate)
Assorted crackers or party breads

TIPS FROM OUR TEST KITCHEN: Crush crackers easily in the sealed wrapper. Use a meat mallet or rolling pin and lightly pound the crackers to the desired texture. Unseal the package and use as directed in the recipe.

World's Best Pimiento Cheese

Betty Bagley, Athens, Tennessee

Serves 20 to 24

"This is always requested as my contribution to our family picnics."

¼ cup mayonnaise

One 3-ounce package cream cheese, softened

3 garlic cloves, minced

¼ cup chopped parsley

6 to 8 drops Tabasco sauce

One 2-ounce jar pimientos, undrained

3 cups finely shredded sharp Cheddar

1 cup pecan chips

1. Purée the mayonnaise, cream cheese, garlic, parsley, and Tabasco in a food processor or blender until smooth. Spoon the mixture into a medium bowl. Add the pimientos, Cheddar, and pecans; mix well.

2. Cover with plastic wrap and refrigerate for at least 4 hours to overnight to allow the flavors to blend.

TIPS FROM OUR TEST KITCHEN: It's important to use pecan chips. If they are not available, place whole pecans in a food processor or blender and pulse to a coarse texture. This recipe is great as a spread for sandwiches or served as a cheese ball or log with a variety of crackers.

Sweet Cinnamon Chips with Fruit Salsa

Elaine Fetter, Rittman, Ohio

Serves 3 to 4

"This recipe is delicious. I have made it several times for couple get-togethers and for our combined Thanksgiving-Christmas family get-together."

1. Preheat the oven to 375°F.

2. To prepare the chips, cut each tortilla into 8 wedges. Brush with the melted butter. Place buttered side up in two 15×10-inch jelly roll pans.

3. Combine the cinnamon and sugar in a small bowl; mix well. Sprinkle over the buttered wedges. Bake for 5 minutes, or until the tortillas barely begin to crisp.

4. Place the pans on wire racks to cool completely. The chips will become crisper as they cool.

5. To prepare the salsa, combine the pineapple, apple, and berries in a medium bowl; toss gently. Serve with the chips.

CHIPS

Two 10-inch flour tortillas

3 tablespoons butter, melted

1 teaspoon ground cinnamon

2 tablespoons sugar

SALSA

4 ounces crushed pineapple packed in juice, drained

½ small tart red apple, such as Gala or Braeburn, cored and diced

½ cup seasonal berries, or ½ ripe medium banana

TIPS FROM OUR TEST KITCHEN: Any type of fruit may be substituted for the apple and berries. The crushed pineapple is essential because it keeps the other fruit from browning.

Olive Salsa

Mary Bilke, Eagle River, Wisconsin

Serves 16

"*I* have made this for many get-togethers and always have to double the recipe. I have also learned to bring copies of the recipe with me, because anyone new always asks for one. You can make it spicier by adding more jalapeños or leaving the seeds in."

One 7-ounce jar pimiento-stuffed green olives, drained and coarsely chopped

One 6-ounce can pitted black olives, drained and coarsely chopped

1 large tomato, cored, seeded, and coarsely chopped

1 jalapeño chile, seeded and coarsely chopped

2 garlic cloves, minced

2 tablespoons extra virgin olive oil

2 teaspoons red wine vinegar

4 ounces crumbled feta cheese

Corn scoops, tortilla chips, or bagel chips

1. Combine the olives, tomato, jalapeño, garlic, olive oil, and vinegar in a bowl. Toss gently to blend. Cover with plastic wrap and refrigerate at least 1 hour.

2. At serving time, add the feta cheese and lightly toss. Serve with corn scoops, tortilla chips, or bagel chips.

TIPS FROM OUR TEST KITCHEN: This is the perfect appetizer for olive and feta lovers. It has a bit of "bite" to boot.

Gourmet Pecans

Carol Snyder, Sumner, Iowa

Serves 14 to 16

"*I* was looking for something special to serve during our fiftieth wedding anniversary celebration. I tried lots of recipes for sugared pecans, and none could hold a candle to this recipe. It is like eating pecan pie! My college-aged grandsons love to get them in their care packages."

1. Preheat the oven to 300°F. Coat a 15×10-inch jelly roll pan with nonstick cooking spray.

2. Bring 2 cups water to a boil in a large saucepan. Add the pecans, return to a boil, and continue boiling for 1 minute, stirring constantly. Drain in a colander and run under hot water to rinse well. Shake off the excess water and place the pecans on paper towels to absorb the water; pat dry.

3. Place the pecans in a single layer in the prepared pan. Sprinkle with the sugar and mix gently. Drizzle evenly with the butter. Bake for 15 minutes. Stir and bake for 10 to 15 minutes longer, until browned. Cool on a wire rack.

4. Season the cooled pecans with the salt. Remove from the pan with a slotted spoon to an airtight container. Store in the refrigerator. The pecans will keep for several months.

3½ cups pecan halves

½ cup sugar

¼ cup (½ stick) butter, melted

⅛ teaspoon salt

Spicy Snack Mix

Page Gray, Duncan, Oklahoma

Serves 24

"*I* created this snack mix because I was tired of making the traditional party mix. I decided to use other items that I liked. The roasting pan works great for this because it will hold a lot. I fix this recipe at Christmas, put it in decorated tins, and give it as gifts. My family and friends love it for snacking, especially while we watch football games."

½ cup (1 stick) butter or margarine

4 teaspoons chili powder

1 teaspoon garlic salt

1 teaspoon garlic powder

1 teaspoon onion salt

1 teaspoon Spice Island's Beau Monde Seasoning, optional

4 cups Crispix

2 cups Bugles

2 cups small corn chips

2 cups mini cheese-flavored crackers

2 cups pizza- or cheese-flavored goldfish crackers

¼ cup grated Parmesan

1. Preheat the oven to 250°F. Melt the butter in the oven in a roasting pan.

2. Remove the pan from the oven and stir in the spices. Add the Crispix, Bugles, corn chips, cheese crackers, and goldfish crackers; mix well to coat with the butter and seasonings.

3. Bake for 15 minutes. Add the Parmesan and stir to coat well. Bake for 30 minutes longer, or until golden brown, stirring after 15 minutes. Cool completely.

4. Store in tightly covered containers. The mix freezes well in containers or zip-top plastic freezer bags.

Buffalo Wings

Diane McCrory, Trinity, Texas

Serves 5 to 6

"At family reunions, buffalo wings make the best appetizer. They go well with steaks, poultry, or fish. They are so easy to make—you may even forget they're cooking. These hot wings are ATOMIC!"

1. Pour the oil into a Dutch oven and place over medium-high heat until hot, about 400°F. Line a baking sheet with paper towels.

2. Add half of the wing pieces to the hot oil and cook until dark golden brown, 15 to 25 minutes. Remove to the baking sheet to drain. Repeat with the remaining wings. Cool.

3. To prepare the sauce, melt the butter in a small saucepan over medium heat. Add the hot sauce, Tabasco, and cayenne. Cook for 2 minutes, or until thoroughly heated, stirring frequently. Reduce the heat to low and keep the sauce warm until serving time.

4. To prepare the dressing, combine the blue cheese, buttermilk, sour cream, mayonnaise, lemon juice, salt, and black pepper in a small bowl. Stir until well blended.

5. Place half of the wings in a gallon-size zip-top plastic bag. Pour half of the sauce over the wings and seal tightly. Turn the bag to coat the wings completely with the sauce. Repeat with the remaining wings.

6. Remove the wings from the bag, and place on a serving platter. Serve immediately with the dressing and the celery.

2 quarts canola or vegetable oil
3½ pounds chicken wings, split at each joint, tips discarded

SAUCE
¼ cup (½ stick) unsalted butter
1 cup hot pepper sauce, such as Frank's Red Hot Sauce
2½ teaspoons Tabasco sauce
1½ teaspoons cayenne pepper, or to taste

DRESSING
2 ounces blue cheese, crumbled
¼ cup buttermilk
¼ cup sour cream
¼ cup mayonnaise
1½ teaspoons lemon juice, or to taste
⅛ teaspoon kosher salt
⅛ teaspoon black pepper

1 bunch celery, trimmed

Stuffed Jalapeños

Denise Bradley, Bowling Green, Kentucky

Serves 8 to 10

"*I*t seems like I can never make enough of this great appetizer. I often use hot sausage, or leave a small amount of the chile membrane in for those who like the chiles a little spicy or hot in flavor."

1 pound bulk pork sausage

One 8-ounce package cream cheese, softened

1 cup grated Parmesan

1¼ pounds jalapeño chiles (about 14)

1. Preheat the oven to 400°F.

2. Heat a large nonstick skillet over medium-high heat. Add the sausage and cook until browned, about 3 minutes, breaking up with a fork and stirring constantly. Remove from the skillet, drain on paper towels, and return to the skillet. Add the cream cheese and Parmesan and stir until well blended.

3. Cut the jalapeños lengthwise and remove the seeds and membranes. Stuff each chile half with the sausage mixture and arrange on a baking pan.

4. Bake for 25 minutes, or until the chiles are tender and the sausage mixture is golden. Remove from the oven and let stand for 10 minutes before serving.

TIPS FROM OUR TEST KITCHEN: Jalapeños can be spicy. Trim, seed, and remove the membranes under cold running water or wear rubber gloves to protect your skin.

Spicy Island Shrimp

JoAnn Geary, Whispering Pines, North Carolina

Serves 12 to 16

"*T*his is a favorite family recipe. I brought a bowl of Spicy Island Shrimp to a Christmas party to share with friends and guests. It disappeared from the serving table shortly after my arrival. The following year, my identical offering to my friend's party never appeared on the serving table. When asked about this situation, the friend said he enjoyed it so much he kept it for himself rather than share it with his guests. It became a Christmas gift to him from then on."

1. Combine the mayonnaise, chili sauce, black pepper, salt, garlic, and cayenne in a bowl; mix well. Add the remaining ingredients and toss to coat.

2. Arrange on a lettuce-lined platter or in a bowl and serve immediately for a pungent flavor or cover with plastic wrap and refrigerate for 8 hours for a more blended flavor. Lobster or chicken may be substituted for the shrimp.

1 cup mayonnaise

⅓ to ½ cup chili sauce

¼ teaspoon black pepper

1 teaspoon salt

1 large garlic clove, minced

⅛ teaspoon cayenne pepper

2 pounds cooked large shrimp, chilled

2 medium green onions, finely chopped

⅓ cup finely chopped red bell pepper

2 tablespoons capers, drained and finely chopped

2 tablespoons prepared horseradish, well drained

Teriyaki Sticks

Mary Ann Jenkins, Gridley, California

Serves 8 to 10

"When our children were small, we lived in the Hawaiian Islands. Our new friends there introduced us to Teriyaki Sticks, which were served at many outdoor get-togethers. When we returned to the mainland, we served Teriyaki Sticks to our friends and families. They all loved them."

1⅓ to 1½ pounds flank steak, about
    1 inch thick
½ to ¾ cup low-sodium or regular soy
    sauce
½ cup sugar
1 teaspoon grated fresh ginger, optional
1 garlic clove, minced, optional
8-inch bamboo skewers, soaked in water
    for 30 minutes

1. Cut the flank steak into thin slices or have a butcher slice it. Combine the soy sauce and sugar in a gallon-size zip-top plastic bag. Add the ginger and garlic, if using. Add the sliced steak and seal tightly.

2. Turn the bag to coat the beef with the teriyaki sauce. Open the bag to release any air inside and re-seal. Refrigerate for up to 48 hours, turning the bag occasionally.

3. Preheat the broiler or grill to high. Thread the flank steak on the skewers, weaving the slices in an "s" pattern.

4. Cook for 2 minutes on each side, or until the flank steak reaches the desired degree of doneness. Do not overcook or the beef will be tough.

Spinach and Artichoke Dip

Eric Helfrich, Wilkes-Barre, Pennsylvania

Serves 25 to 30

"This recipe was a smash at our last family Christmas get-together."

1. Preheat the oven to 400°F. Grease a 13×19-inch baking dish.

2. Combine the spinach, cream cheese, and mayonnaise in a bowl; mix well. Add the drained artichoke hearts, Parmesan, Cheddar, milk, and garlic and stir to thoroughly blend. Add ¼ to ½ cup of the reserved artichoke liquid for the desired consistency.

3. Spread the mixture evenly in the prepared dish. Sprinkle with the French fried onions. Bake for 20 minutes, or until the mixture is lightly browned and bubbly. Serve with baguette slices.

Two 10-ounce packages frozen chopped spinach, thawed and squeezed dry

Two 8-ounce packages cream cheese, softened

1 cup mayonnaise

Two 7-ounce jars marinated artichoke hearts, drained, ½ cup of the liquid reserved

¾ cup grated Parmesan

½ cup shredded sharp Cheddar

¼ cup milk

4 garlic cloves, minced

1 cup French's Original French Fried Onions

2 baguettes, cut into ¼-inch slices

TIPS FROM OUR TEST KITCHEN: For a less creamy consistency, omit 4 ounces of the cream cheese and ¼ cup of the mayonnaise.

Taco Dip

Michelle Worthington, Winchester, Kentucky

Serves 10 to 12

"*T*his dip is a favorite among all my family and friends—even the picky ones. There is always a spot left on the table for my Taco Dip at any get-together. Everyone enjoys the taste, color, and how easy it is to make."

One 8-ounce package cream cheese, softened
One 16-ounce container sour cream
½ cup mild salsa
One 1-ounce envelope mild taco seasoning mix
One 1-ounce envelope onion soup mix
4 cups shredded lettuce
3 cups shredded Mexican-style cheese
3 medium tomatoes, chopped
1 cup French's Original French Fried Onions, coarsely crushed, optional
Tortilla chips

1. Combine the cream cheese, sour cream, salsa, taco seasoning mix, and onion soup mix in a medium bowl. Blend well with a mixer at low speed.

2. Spoon the mixture into a shallow pasta bowl or 13×9-inch baking dish. Using the back of a spoon, smooth the surface. Sprinkle the lettuce over the cream cheese mixture. Top with the cheese and tomatoes. For added crunch, add French fried onions to the top before serving, if using. Serve with tortilla chips.

TIPS FROM OUR TEST KITCHEN: When scooping with the tortilla chips, be sure to dip down to the bottom layer. This dip may be made several days in advance, but do not top with the lettuce, tomatoes, cheese, and French fried onions until 2 hours prior to serving for peak texture.

Breads

A cherished bread recipe can be a cook's pride and joy and a much anticipated part of a get-together with family or friends.

Judith Collier Wright of Lake Almanor, California, has gained quite a reputation for Mom's Magic Muffins. She says she'd better not arrive at a church potluck or family gathering without them. Wright is always prepared to bake a batch of her healthful muffins—she keeps batter in her refrigerator.

Oats and whole wheat flour give Mary Ann Kauchak's Cranberry Bread with Orange and Oats a good-for-you advantage. Kauchak, of Woodbridge, Virginia, made a point of coming up with healthful ingredients for her moist, tart bread that packs a punch of flavor.

Wanda Taylor of Gould, Oklahoma, has won votes of approval from family and church friends for her sweet Monkey Bread. It has also won top honors more than once at the Harmon County Fair. It's hard to resist the sweet cinnamon-sugar flavor of the tasty yeast bread.

The name of Dorothy Coverston's Tex-Mex Corn Bread Special says it all. The Coeur d'Alene, Idaho, resident, who combined several recipes handed down from her ninety-two-year-old mother to come up with her own version, says it's good for a crowd or for a small get-together with friends or family.

And at the Ogden, Utah, home of Melanie Myrtle Wilhelmsen, the next generation of bakers is learning to knead dough and prepare breads. Although three-year-old Ella Myrtle Wilhelmsen probably isn't a fan of Simon & Garfunkel yet, she enjoys helping her mother add the parsley, sage, rosemary, and thyme to the batter for Scarborough Fair Herb Bread. Wilhelmsen takes the savory treat to once-a-month dinners at her parents' home where her eight siblings eagerly wait to taste it.

Mom's Magic Muffins

Judith Collier Wright, Lake Almanor, California

Makes 4 dozen

"I'd better not show up at a church potluck or a family gathering without a basket of warm muffins. There is always batter in my refrigerator. They are good with any meal or as a snack. Kids love them, and don't realize they are eating healthy food."

1. Combine the cereal, flour, sugar, baking soda, and salt in a large bowl; mix well. Mix the buttermilk, oil, and eggs in a separate large bowl and whisk well. Pour the egg mixture into the cereal mixture and stir until just blended. Fold in the cranberries.

2. Store in a tightly covered container in the refrigerator. The batter will keep for six weeks and improves over time. Do not stir at any time after refrigerating or when preparing to bake the muffins.

3. Preheat the oven to 400°F. Grease muffin tins. Carefully spoon the batter into the prepared pan. Bake for 18 minutes, or until a wooden pick inserted in the center comes out almost clean. Cool in the muffin tins for 10 minutes. Serve warm or remove to a wire rack to cool completely.

One 14-ounce box Raisin Bran cereal
5 cups all-purpose flour
3 cups sugar
5 teaspoons baking soda
2 teaspoons salt
1 quart buttermilk
1 cup vegetable oil
4 eggs, beaten
1½ cups dried, sweetened cranberries

TIPS FROM OUR TEST KITCHEN: These muffins freeze well.

Easy Banana Bread

Lea Fiore, Marble, North Carolina

Serves 16

"My brother frequently takes friends rafting on the Ocoee River on Sundays. There's usually an after-rafting party at his house. We like to grill food and bake this banana bread. This is an easy, one-bowl recipe."

½ cup (1 stick) butter, softened

¾ cup sugar

2 eggs

1 teaspoon vanilla extract

1½ cups all-purpose flour

½ teaspoon salt

1 teaspoon baking soda

2 ripe bananas, mashed

½ cup chopped pecans, walnuts, or chocolate chips

1 cup sour cream

1. Preheat the oven to 350°F. Grease an 8×4-inch loaf pan.

2. Cream the butter and sugar in a large bowl with a mixer at medium-high speed. Add the eggs and vanilla and beat until well blended.

3. Combine the flour, salt, and baking soda in a medium bowl. Add to the butter mixture. Add the bananas, pecans, and sour cream. Mix until just blended.

4. Pour the batter into the prepared pan and bake for 1 hour, or until a wooden pick inserted in the center comes out almost clean. Cool in the pan for 15 minutes and remove to a wire rack to cool completely.

Cranberry Bread with Orange and Oats

Mary Ann Kauchak, Woodbridge, Virginia

Serves 18

"*T*his tart, dense bread is moist with fruit and great for breakfast or tea time with the girls. Eat it plain, or enhance it with a bit of whipped cream cheese."

1. Preheat the oven to 350°F.

2. Combine the eggs and brown sugar in a food processor and purée until smooth. Add the oil and diced orange. Process until the orange is minced. Gradually add the orange juice and pulse until smooth.

3. Mix the oats, all-purpose flour, whole wheat flour, baking powder, baking soda, and salt in a large bowl. Stir in the orange mixture until just blended. Let stand for 15 minutes.

4. Combine the cranberries and 2 cups hot water in a medium bowl. Let stand for 10 minutes. Drain well, shaking off any excess liquid.

5. Fold the cranberries into the batter. Pour into a 9×5-inch loaf pan. Bake for 50 to 55 minutes, until a wooden pick inserted in the center comes out almost clean. Cool in the pan for 15 minutes and remove to a wire rack to cool completely. Serve with whipped cream cheese, if using.

2 eggs
1 cup packed light brown sugar
3 tablespoons vegetable oil
1 medium orange, diced with skin
¾ cup orange juice
1 cup quick-cooking oats
1 cup all-purpose flour
1 cup whole wheat flour
1 tablespoon baking powder
½ teaspoon baking soda
¾ teaspoon salt
1½ cups dried, sweetened cranberries
Whipped cream cheese, optional

TIPS FROM OUR TEST KITCHEN: For a moister texture, increase the amount of vegetable oil to ⅓ cup.

Zucchini Carrot Bread

Libby Carlsten, Los Alamos, New Mexico

Serves 32

"**S**everal times I've taken this bread to our office staff meeting, and people seem to love it."

2 eggs

1 cup vegetable oil

2 cups sugar

1 cup grated zucchini (1 medium)

1 cup grated carrots (2 medium)

2 teaspoons vanilla extract

2 cups all-purpose flour

$\frac{1}{2}$ teaspoon baking soda

$1\frac{1}{2}$ teaspoons baking powder

1 tablespoon ground cinnamon

$\frac{1}{2}$ teaspoon salt

$\frac{1}{2}$ cup shredded coconut

1 cup chopped pecans or walnuts

1. Preheat the oven to 350°F. Grease two 8×4-inch loaf pans.

2. Beat the eggs in a large bowl. Add the oil, sugar, zucchini, carrots, and vanilla; mix well. Sift the dry ingredients and add to the egg mixture. Stir until just blended.

3. Fold in the coconut and pecans. Divide the mixture between the two prepared pans.

4. Bake for 1 hour, or until a wooden pick inserted in the center comes out almost clean. Cool in the pans for 15 minutes. Remove to a wire rack to cool completely.

TIPS FROM OUR TEST KITCHEN: This bread makes its own crunchy topping.

Tex-Mex Corn Bread Special

Dorothy Coverston, Coeur d'Alene, Idaho

Serves 18 to 24

"*I* combined several recipes given to me by my ninety-two-year-old mother to make my own Tex-Mex Corn Bread Special. I have served this treasure to large crowds and for small get-togethers, with never a crumb left for me! I like it best with chili."

1. Preheat the oven to 350°F. Grease and flour a 13×9-inch baking dish.

2. Combine the eggs and oil in a large bowl; whisk to blend. Add the creamed corn, whole kernel corn, pimientos, chiles, onion, and salt. Stir in the Cheddar. Add the corn bread mix and stir until just blended. Spoon into the prepared pan.

3. Bake for 45 minutes, or until a wooden pick inserted in the center comes out clean. Top with sour cream and French fried onions, if using.

4 eggs
1 cup vegetable oil
One 14-ounce can creamed corn
One 15-ounce can whole kernel corn, drained
One 7-ounce jar sliced pimientos, drained
One 4-ounce can chopped green chiles
2 tablespoons minced onion
½ teaspoon salt
8 ounces sharp Cheddar, shredded (2 cups)
One 19-ounce box corn bread mix
Sour cream, optional
French's Original French Fried Onions, optional

Butterhorns

Bonita Martin, Danville, Pennsylvania

Makes 32 rolls

"*T*his recipe was my mother-in-law's. Butterhorns are soft and fluffy and almost melt in your mouth."

One ¼-ounce package active dry yeast

½ cup plus 1 tablespoon sugar

3 eggs, well beaten

½ cup (1 stick) plus 2 tablespoons butter or margarine, melted

1 teaspoon salt

4½ cups all-purpose flour

1. Dissolve the yeast and 1 tablespoon of the sugar in 1 cup warm (115°F) water in a small bowl. Stir with a wooden spoon.

2. Combine the eggs, ½ cup of the melted butter, the salt, and the remaining ½ cup sugar in a large bowl; beat well. Add the yeast mixture to the egg mixture. Stir in 3 cups of the flour and beat hard with a wooden spoon. Quickly work in the remaining 1½ cups flour. The dough will be quite soft. Cover the bowl with plastic wrap and refrigerate overnight.

3. Divide the dough into 4 sections. Roll each section into a 12- to 14-inch circle. Brush with the remaining 2 tablespoons melted butter. Cut each round into 8 wedges. Roll up, starting at the large end, and shape into crescents. Place on greased baking sheets and cover with plastic wrap. Let rise in a warm place until doubled in size, or 2 to 4 hours.

4. Preheat the oven to 375°F. Bake for 12 to 15 minutes, until lightly browned. Serve warm.

TIPS FROM OUR TEST KITCHEN: It is easy to have these warm rolls on the dinner table because the work is divided over two days.

Monkey Bread

Wanda Taylor, Gould, Oklahoma

"I have served my Monkey Bread at family get-togethers, church dinners, and special suppers, as well as at home. It has won first prize—more than once—at the Harmon County Fair!"

1. Scald the milk in a small saucepan. Add ⅓ cup of the sugar, ⅓ cup of the butter, and the salt. Heat until the butter melts and the sugar dissolves. Remove from the heat and cool to lukewarm.

2. Dissolve the yeast in ¼ cup lukewarm (110 to 115°F) water in a large bowl. Stir in the eggs and milk mixture. Stir in 2 cups of the flour; beat until smooth. Add 2 additional cups of the flour; mix well. If the dough seems too wet, add another ½ cup flour. Cover and let rise until doubled in size. Punch the dough down and let it rise again until doubled in size.

3. Combine the remaining 1½ cups sugar and the cinnamon in a small bowl; blend well. Melt the remaining ¾ cup butter in a microwave-safe bowl. Place the pecans in a small bowl. Roll the dough into walnut-size balls. (If the dough is too wet to handle easily, scoop up a portion of dough with a soup spoon.) Dip the balls into the melted butter, then in the sugar mixture, then in the pecans. Pile the balls loosely in an ungreased Bundt pan. Let rise for 40 minutes.

4. Preheat the oven to 400°F. Bake the bread for 10 minutes and reduce the heat to 325°F. Bake for 25 minutes longer. Remove from the oven and invert immediately onto a serving plate. Serve hot. Do not cut; let diners "pluck" a serving.

1 cup milk

1½ cups plus ⅓ cup sugar

¾ cup (1½ sticks) plus ⅓ cup butter

½ teaspoon salt

One ¼-ounce package active dry yeast

3 eggs, well beaten

4 to 4½ cups all-purpose flour

2 to 3 tablespoons ground cinnamon

1¼ cups pecans, ground

Featherbed Potato Rolls

Phyllis Biggs, Dobson, North Carolina

Makes 24 rolls

"*T*his is a favorite for Thanksgiving and Christmas family dinners. I have made these rolls for more than forty years. They are so easy and are foolproof. Nothing smells better than fresh yeast bread rising. At our family dinners, each plate will usually have at least two of these giant hot rolls."

1 medium baking potato
One ¼-ounce package active dry yeast
⅓ cup sugar
1½ teaspoons salt
**¼ cup (½ stick) plus 2 tablespoons
    butter or margarine, softened**
1 egg, beaten
4½ cups all-purpose flour

TIPS FROM OUR TEST KITCHEN: Potato rolls usually rise slowly. During the lengthy rising, they develop flavor.

1. Place the potato in a small saucepan with water to cover. Cook until tender. Remove the potato, cool slightly, and peel. Reserve ¾ cup of the potato water.

2. Dissolve the yeast in ¼ cup warm (115°F) water in a bowl. Mash the potato with a fork to yield ½ cup.

3. Combine the sugar, salt, and ¼ cup of the softened butter in a bowl. Add the reserved potato water; mix well. Cool to lukewarm and add the yeast mixture, the mashed potato, egg, and 2 cups of the flour; stir until smooth.

4. Add 2 additional cups of the flour or more as needed to make a smooth, soft dough. Turn out on a lightly floured board and knead until smooth, about 5 minutes. Turn the dough into a well-greased bowl; turn to grease the top. Cover and let rise until doubled in size, 1 to 1½ hours.

5. Punch the dough down, divide in half and shape each half into 12 smooth balls. Arrange on a greased baking sheet. Melt the remaining 2 tablespoons butter in a microwave-safe bowl. Brush the rolls with the melted butter. Let rise for 1 to 1½ hours.

6. Preheat the oven to 375°F. Bake for 15 minutes, or until golden.

Scarborough Fair Herb Bread

Melanie Myrtle Wilhelmsen, Ogden, Utah

Serves 32

"*M*y three-year-old daughter, Ella Myrtle, loves to cook with me, especially homemade bread. We take it to church potlucks, work parties, and, of course, family get-togethers. Our extended family especially loves our herb bread. I have eight siblings and most of us meet for dinner at my parents' house once a month."

1. Combine 4 cups of the flour, the sugar, salt, yeast, and 2½ cups very warm (120 to 130°F) water in a large bowl. Add the herbs and stir until well blended. Stir in the remaining flour until smooth. Cover and let rise until doubled in size, about 45 minutes.

2. Grease two 9×5-inch loaf pans with the shortening.

3. Stir the dough for 25 strokes. Divide between the prepared pans. Cover and let rise until doubled in size, 30 to 45 minutes.

4. Preheat the oven to 375°F.

5. Bake the loaves for 30 minutes. Reduce the heat to 350°F and bake for 15 minutes longer, or until the bread sounds hollow when tapped on the bottom. Cover the loaves loosely with foil during the last 10 minutes of baking time if needed to prevent overbrowning. Remove from the pans immediately and brush with melted butter. Cool on a wire rack.

6 cups all-purpose flour

2 tablespoons sugar

2 teaspoons salt

2½ tablespoons active dry yeast

3 tablespoons dried parsley, or more to taste

½ teaspoon or more rubbed sage

1¼ teaspoons or more dried rosemary

1 teaspoon or more dried thyme

2 tablespoons vegetable shortening

Melted butter

> *TIPS FROM OUR TEST KITCHEN:* Serve the bread warm with extra virgin olive oil for dipping to bring out the flavors. Use fresh herbs if desired by tripling the amounts given for dried.

Soups

Soup is a friend to the busy home cook, since it often can be prepared ahead of time. When company comes to call, the soup is ready to be rewarmed and served with ease. And since there's nothing more comforting than a steaming bowl of soup on a cold day, soup can bring a family together for a casual meal. It's also perfect for serving to a houseful of guests or a high-school gym full of revelers.

Kimberly Hammond of Kingwood, Texas, enjoys preparing her tasty No-Soak Black Bean Soup not only because it cooks all day in a slow cooker, but also because the dried beans don't have to be soaked.

Cheeseburger Soup is as much a part of the Thanksgiving get-together for Beverly Kivett of Madras, Oregon, as the turkey and dressing. Her family looks forward to having a bowl of the filling soup with some yummy bread the night before the big holiday.

Sheryl Crumpton of Lindale, Texas, has a hit on her hands when she fixes Incredible Chicken Tortilla Soup to take to a church potluck dinner or family event. The name says it all—this hearty, flavorful soup filled with chicken, beans, and spices, looks as good as it tastes.

On a frigid day, Sue Brintle headed to her pantry to create a rib-sticking chili that would warm her husband and daughter from the inside out. Brintle, of Mount Airy, North Carolina, didn't have any ground beef or turkey, but came up with Healthy Vegetable Chili, loaded with beans, corn, tomatoes, and other vegetables.

Roasted Eggplant Soup with Garlic Cream from Lillian Julow of Gainesville, Florida, and Superb Red Pepper Soup, submitted by Eleanor Greenly of Levittown, Pennsylvania, both take advantage of fresh produce and spices to create gourmet dishes that burst with flavor.

And for Elaine Stieber of Norwalk, Ohio, it's a matter of great pride that her French Onion Soup is her husband's favorite. He loves to order the soup in restaurants but says no one makes it better than his wife of fifteen years. She says he's her biggest fan—and adds, "You can't beat that!"

Glazed Apple Bars (page 168)

Quick Apple Dumplings (page 196)

Shrimp Basil (page 156)

Blackberry Cake (page 176)

Broccoli Elegant (page 87)

Butterhorns (page 46)

Champagne Brunch Casserole (page 10)

Cherry Glazed Pork Roast (page 147)   *Incredible Chicken Tortilla Soup (page 56)*

Fudge Cappuccino Orange Torte (page 198)

Sweet Cinnamon Chips with Fruit Salsa (page 29)

Homestyle Grits Casserole (page 94)

Goat Cheese Torte (page 26)

Dish of Fire (page 103)

Garden Corn and Black Bean Salad (page 68)

Midnight Biscotti (page 169)

Monkey Bread (page 47)

No-Soak Black Bean Soup

Kimberly Hammond, Kingwood, Texas

Serves 8

*"T*his recipe is especially easy because you don't soak the beans. You can put everything in the slow cooker in the morning and forget about it for the rest of the day."

1. Add the olive oil to a 5-quart slow cooker and turn it to the highest setting. Stir in the yellow onion and cook for 5 minutes. Add the green bell pepper to the slow cooker with the garlic, black beans, 5 cups hot water, vegetable broth, chiles, 2 teaspoons of the cumin, thyme, salt, pepper, and bay leaves. Cover and cook on high for at least 8 hours.

2. Remove the bay leaves. Before serving, blend with a hand mixer or hand-held submersible blender until the mixture is thick, with beans, onion, and peppers visible. Add the remaining 1 teaspoon cumin.

3. Ladle into soup bowls and top each serving with a dollop of sour cream and 1 teaspoon each of the red bell pepper and white onion. Sprinkle with the cilantro.

1 tablespoon olive oil

1 medium yellow onion, chopped

1 medium green bell pepper, cut into 1-inch pieces

7 garlic cloves, minced

1 pound dried black beans, rinsed and drained

3 cups vegetable broth

Two 4-ounce cans chopped green chiles

1 tablespoon ground cumin

1 teaspoon dried thyme

1 teaspoon salt

½ teaspoon black pepper

2 bay leaves

½ cup nondairy soy sour cream or plain sour cream

½ medium red bell pepper, finely chopped

½ medium white onion, finely chopped

¼ cup finely chopped cilantro

Black-Eyed Pea Soup

Pat Tomme, Brownwood, Texas

Serves 10

"This is my family's favorite around a good campfire or the dining table."

1 pound bulk pork sausage

1 medium onion, chopped

½ cup chopped celery, optional

Four 15-ounce cans black-eyed peas, undrained

One 14-ounce can diced tomatoes

One 10-ounce can diced tomatoes with green chiles, undrained

2 tablespoons chili powder

1. Heat a Dutch oven over medium-high heat. Add the sausage, onion, and celery, if using. Cook until the onion is translucent and the sausage is no longer pink, stirring constantly.

2. Add the black-eyed peas, tomatoes, tomatoes with green chiles, and chili powder. Bring to a boil, reduce the heat and simmer, covered, for 30 minutes, or until the onion is tender. Ladle into soup bowls.

TIPS FROM OUR TEST KITCHEN: Freeze leftovers in zip-top plastic freezer sandwich bags for individual servings. This is an easy, rib-sticking, comfort soup that's great served with corn bread.

Cheeseburger Soup

Beverly Kivett, Madras, Oregon

"*O*ur family likes to have Cheeseburger Soup the night before Thanksgiving, when a bowl of hot soup and some yummy bread is just right. It can be made ahead of time and then put in a slow cooker for easy serving."

1. Heat a stockpot over medium-high heat. Add the ground beef and cook until browned, stirring frequently. Remove the beef and set aside. Drain the pot.

2. Heat the oil in the stockpot. Add the onion, carrots, celery, basil, and parsley. Cook for 4 minutes, stirring frequently. Increase the heat to high. Add the broth and potatoes, and return the ground beef to the pot. Reduce the heat, cover, and simmer for 10 to 15 minutes, until the potatoes are tender.

3. Add the milk, salt, and pepper and cook for 2 to 3 minutes longer to heat thoroughly. Remove from the heat, add the cheese, and stir until melted. Blend in the sour cream.

1½ pounds ground beef

1 tablespoon vegetable oil

1 large onion, chopped

2 medium carrots, shredded

2 medium celery stalks, diced

1 teaspoon dried basil

1 teaspoon dried parsley

5 cups chicken broth

4 medium potatoes, peeled and diced

3 cups milk

1½ teaspoons salt, or to taste

½ teaspoon black pepper

4 to 6 cups shredded Colby Jack cheese

1 cup sour cream

Incredible Chicken Tortilla Soup

Sheryl Crumpton, Lindale, Texas

Serves 12

*"T*his soup is absolutely wonderful! It is a very pretty dish that tastes as good as it looks. It is always a big hit when I bring it to brunch get-togethers, church potlucks, or family events. Be sure to bring the recipe, because you'll be asked for it!"

2 tablespoons olive oil

1 large onion, chopped

2 medium carrots, finely chopped

2 tablespoons minced garlic

3 cups chicken broth

One 14-ounce can diced tomatoes, undrained

1 cup mild picante sauce

One 15-ounce can Ranch-Style Beans, undrained

One 15-ounce can black beans, rinsed and drained

1 cup frozen whole kernel corn

1 teaspoon ground cumin

½ teaspoon black pepper

½ teaspoon dried oregano

½ teaspoon chili powder

⅛ teaspoon paprika

2 cups chopped cooked chicken

¼ cup chopped cilantro

Tortilla chips

Sliced avocados

Shredded Cheddar

1. Heat the olive oil in a Dutch oven over medium heat. Add the onion, carrots, and garlic. Cook until the onion is tender, about 6 minutes.

2. Increase the heat to high and add the broth, tomatoes, picante sauce, beans, corn, and spices. Bring to a boil, reduce the heat, cover, and simmer for 30 minutes. Add the chicken and cilantro. Cook until thoroughly heated.

3. Ladle into soup bowls and top with tortilla chips, sliced avocados, and shredded Cheddar.

TIPS FROM OUR TEST KITCHEN: If not serving immediately, add the cilantro at serving time for peak flavor. Substitute canned pinto beans for the ranch-style beans, if desired.

Healthy Vegetable Chili

Sue Brintle, Mount Airy, North Carolina

Serves 14

"*O*ne really cold day I wanted chili but didn't have any ground beef or turkey. I used what I had on hand and came up with this recipe. My husband and daughter loved it, so I wrote it down. When it is cold, we like something that warms us from the inside out."

1. Heat the oil in a stockpot over medium heat. Add the onion and garlic and cook until the onion is translucent, about 4 minutes, stirring frequently. Increase the heat to high and add the remaining ingredients.

2. Bring to a boil, reduce the heat, and simmer, uncovered, stirring frequently, until the vegetables are tender and flavors are blended, about 40 minutes.

2 tablespoons canola or olive oil

1 medium onion, chopped

2 garlic cloves, minced

1 medium celery stalk, sliced

1 medium carrot, chopped

2 cups whole kernel corn

Three 15-ounce cans black beans, rinsed and drained

One 15-ounce can kidney beans, rinsed and drained

Two 14-ounce cans diced tomatoes, undrained

One 10-ounce can diced tomatoes with green chiles, undrained

1 cup medium salsa

1/2 cup ketchup

One 14-ounce can beef or chicken broth

1 tablespoon Worcestershire sauce

One 1-ounce package chili seasoning

1 teaspoon chili powder

1 teaspoon ground cumin

1/4 teaspoon paprika

TIPS FROM OUR TEST KITCHEN: Top the chili with sour cream, shredded Cheddar, or tortilla chips, if desired. Or spoon the chili on top of a baked potato or a bed of cooked brown rice. Flavors improve if the chili is refrigerated overnight. It also freezes well.

Clam Chowder

Judy Lehmann, Ida Grove, Iowa

Serves 10

"We enjoyed eating clam chowder when traveling out West, but no one would give us their recipe, so I came up with this version myself. My friends ask me to let them know when I'm going to make it so they can come visit at suppertime."

10 small red potatoes, chopped (about 5 cups)
Three 8-ounce bottles clam juice
½ cup finely chopped onions
½ cup finely chopped celery
One 14-ounce can sliced carrots, drained and chopped
½ cup chopped cooked bacon or bacon bits
½ teaspoon dried basil
½ teaspoon dried oregano
¼ teaspoon dried thyme
2 teaspoons salt, or to taste
¼ teaspoon black pepper, or to taste
½ cup (1 stick) butter or margarine
½ cup all-purpose flour
2 cups half-and-half
Three 6-ounce cans minced clams, rinsed and well drained

1. Combine the potatoes, clam juice, and ¼ cup of the onion in a Dutch oven. Add the celery, carrots, bacon, herbs, salt, and pepper. Bring to a boil over high heat. Reduce the heat and simmer, uncovered, until the potatoes are tender, about 15 minutes.

2. Melt the butter in a medium saucepan over medium heat. Add the remaining ¼ cup onion and cook until soft, about 5 minutes. Whisk in the flour. Remove from the heat and slowly whisk in the half-and-half, mixing until smooth.

3. Heat the cream mixture over medium heat, whisking until thickened. Add the clams and cream mixture to the potato mixture. Cook, uncovered, over low heat for 15 minutes, stirring occasionally.

TIPS FROM OUR TEST KITCHEN: For a thinner consistency, stir in an additional cup of half-and-half.

Cream of Crab Soup

Audie Goddard, Glen Burnie, Maryland

Serves 12

1. Melt the butter in a Dutch oven over medium-low heat. Gradually stir in the flour, whisking until smooth. Add the evaporated milk slowly, whisking until smooth.

2. Stir in the half-and-half gradually to achieve a smooth consistency. Increase the heat to medium and stir constantly with a flat spatula as the soup thickens. Add the seafood seasoning, parsley, salt, and pepper. Add the crabmeat, stirring gently. Cook until thoroughly heated.

½ cup (1 stick) butter

1 cup all-purpose flour

One 5-ounce can evaporated milk

2 quarts half-and-half

2 to 4 teaspoons seafood seasoning

½ to 1 teaspoon dried parsley

1 teaspoon salt, or to taste

⅛ to ¼ teaspoon black pepper

1 pound fresh crabmeat, picked over for shells and cartilage

Roasted Eggplant Soup with Garlic Cream

Lillian Julow, Gainesville, Florida

2 medium eggplants

2 pounds fresh plum tomatoes

½ cup extra virgin olive oil

2 medium unpeeled garlic cloves

1 medium onion, chopped

1 medium red bell pepper, seeded and
    chopped

1 medium green bell pepper, seeded and
    chopped

7 cups vegetable or chicken broth

3 tablespoons chopped basil, or
    1 tablespoon dried basil

3 tablespoons chopped oregano, or
    1 tablespoon dried oregano

3 tablespoons chopped parsley

2 cups sour cream or crème fraîche

Salt and pepper

1. Preheat the oven to 425°F. Rinse the eggplants and tomatoes and pat dry. Cut the eggplants lengthwise. Brush the cut sides of the eggplants with ¼ cup of the olive oil. Place the eggplants, tomatoes, and garlic on a large foil-lined baking sheet. Bake for 35 minutes, or until soft. Remove from the oven and cool.

2. When the eggplants are cool enough to handle, remove the stems and skin. Coarsely chop the eggplants and tomatoes and reserve any liquid. Gently squeeze out the garlic from the individual cloves into a small bowl.

3. Heat the remaining ¼ cup olive oil in a Dutch oven over medium heat. Add the onion and bell peppers and cook, stirring frequently, until the onion is transparent, 6 to 8 minutes. Add the broth, herbs, eggplants, and tomatoes. Bring to a boil, reduce the heat, and simmer, uncovered, for 30 minutes.

4. Combine the garlic and sour cream in a food processor. Process until smooth. Season with salt and pepper. Taste the soup and adjust the seasonings. Serve in bowls with a dollop of garlic cream on top.

TIPS FROM OUR TEST KITCHEN: To make crème fraîche, whisk 2 cups heavy cream and ½ cup sour cream at room temperature in a large bowl. Cover the bowl with plastic wrap and let stand in a warm, draft-free area for 12 hours to overnight. Store, covered, in the refrigerator for up to two weeks. Serve well chilled.

Slow Cooker Enchilada Soup

Cindy Gilliand, Augusta, Kansas

Serves 6

"My family loved this soup when I fixed it to eat during the Super Bowl. It's a wonderful 'warm-up' on cold days."

1. Combine the chicken, soup, enchilada sauce, chiles, and broth in a slow cooker. Cook on low for 6 hours.

2. Add the cream cheese and whisk until smooth. Top with cilantro or green onions.

2 boneless, skinless chicken breasts, cut into bite-size pieces

One 10-ounce can cream of chicken soup

One 10-ounce can green enchilada sauce

One 4-ounce can chopped green chiles

1 cup chicken broth

One 8-ounce package cream cheese, cut into small cubes, softened

Chopped cilantro or green onions

TIPS FROM OUR TEST KITCHEN: Serve with warm flour tortillas, tortilla chips, or canned French fried onion rings, if desired.

French Onion Soup

Elaine Stieber, Norwalk, Ohio

Serves 6

"I have served this soup to several friends with great success. But my biggest fan is my husband of fifteen years. He often orders onion soup in restaurants but says nobody makes it better than I do. You can't beat that!"

¼ cup (½ stick) butter or margarine

2½ pounds sweet onions, thinly sliced

1 tablespoon all-purpose flour

¼ teaspoon salt, or to taste

One 14-ounce can beef broth

One 14-ounce can chicken broth

½ cup white wine, such as Chardonnay

1½ cups croutons, or to taste

1½ cups shredded mozzarella, or to taste

1. Preheat the oven to 400°F.

2. Melt the butter in a Dutch oven over medium-high heat. Add the onions and cook until they are lightly brown and tender, about 25 minutes, stirring frequently.

3. Stir in the flour and salt. Add the broth, 1 cup water, and the wine. Bring to a boil, reduce the heat, and simmer, uncovered, for 20 minutes to blend flavors.

4. Spoon the mixture into ovenproof soup bowls. Top each serving with croutons and cheese. Place the bowls on a baking sheet. Bake for 10 to 15 minutes, until the cheese melts.

Superb Red Pepper Soup

Eleanor Greenly, Levittown, Pennsylvania

Serves 8

1. Preheat the broiler. Line a large baking sheet or broiler pan with foil.

2. Arrange the bell peppers, cut side down, on the baking sheet. Broil 4 inches from the heat source for 14 minutes, or until the peppers are blackened and blistered.

3. Remove the peppers to a medium bowl. Cover with plastic wrap and let stand for 20 minutes. Peel the peppers, discarding the seeds, skin, and stems; coarsely chop.

4. Melt the butter in a Dutch oven over medium heat. Add the onion and garlic and sauté for 10 minutes, stirring frequently. Stir in the carrots and cook for 10 minutes. Add the bell peppers, potato, pears, and broth. Bring to a boil, reduce the heat, and simmer, uncovered, until the vegetables are tender, about 20 minutes. Add the parsley.

5. Working in 1-cup batches, purée the soup in a blender, holding the lid down firmly. Return the soup to the Dutch oven and reheat over medium heat. Season with salt and pepper.

6. Ladle the soup into individual bowls and garnish with crème fraîche and parsley sprigs.

6 medium red bell peppers, halved

½ cup (1 stick) salted butter

1 large onion, chopped

2 garlic cloves, minced

3 large carrots, peeled and chopped

1 large baking potato, peeled and chopped

2 medium firm pears, peeled, cored, and chopped

One 32-ounce container chicken broth

1 tablespoon chopped parsley

Salt and pepper

½ cup crème fraîche or sour cream

Parsley sprigs

TIPS FROM OUR TEST KITCHEN: The recipe for Crème Fraîche is on page 60.

Salads

*D*uring summer months, farm-fresh corn, tomatoes, bell peppers, and other vegetables star in salads across the country. Traditional coleslaw, and tasty variations, including one with cranberries and walnuts—also are popular on *American Profile* readers' menus. And a flavorful pasta salad is often the perfect complement to fresh-caught fish at potluck suppers.

For her nephew's high school graduation luncheon at his family farm, Ellen Russell decided to take advantage of the sweet corn his parents grow. Although Russell, of LeMars, Iowa, tripled her Garden Corn and Black Bean Salad, it was gone before she ever had a chance to get a portion for herself.

Waneta Stephens of Mount Pulaski, Illinois, had better pack a pen and recipe cards whenever she takes her Easy Coleslaw to a get-together. She says people always request the recipe. When the VFW asked her to prepare the slaw for their ham and bean supper for two hundred, she knew she had a hit on her hands. Her husband cut the cabbage, and she made the dressing. To cap off the evening, Stephens says people purchased the slaw that was left over to take home.

Mary Jaskolka, a Hurricane Katrina evacuee now living in Hot Springs, Arkansas, takes her Buttermilk Coleslaw to gatherings at her new apartment complex. Her neighbors approve of the healthy salad.

Once a month, Linda Bier and her Church Hill Circle of quilters in Hannibal, Missouri, gather to sew, spend time together, and enjoy good food. Her Cranberry Walnut Cabbage Slaw is always welcome. Bier says she has also shared the slaw at family gatherings.

Gloria Stevens of Kingsville, Ohio, pairs her Pasta Pizza Salad with fresh Lake Erie perch and walleye. Living on one of the Great Lakes, she has ample opportunities to fish—and catch the ingredients for a good meal.

Black Bean Couscous Corn Salad

Mary Bullen, Gibsonia, Pennsylvania

Serves 16 to 18

"I used this recipe for a baby shower luncheon for my daughter, who had a little girl in October 2006."

1. Prepare the couscous according to the package directions. To cool quickly, spread the couscous on a large baking sheet in a thin layer and let stand for 10 minutes.

2. Combine the cooled couscous, corn, beans, green onions, bell pepper, and garlic in a bowl; mix gently. Add the lemon juice and olive oil; toss well. Season with salt and pepper.

One 10-ounce package dry plain couscous

One 16-ounce bag frozen white or yellow corn, thawed and drained

One 15-ounce can black beans, rinsed and drained

4 medium green onions, sliced (white and green parts)

1 medium red bell pepper, finely chopped

2 garlic cloves, minced

Juice of 2 lemons (¼ cup)

¼ cup extra virgin olive oil

Salt and pepper

TIPS FROM OUR TEST KITCHEN: Giant pasta pearls, such as Casbah Toasted Couscous, may be used in place of the plain couscous. To enhance the flavor, add a bit of grated lemon zest, minced jalapeño chile, or cilantro.

Garden Corn and Black Bean Salad

Ellen Russell, LeMars, Iowa

Serves 8

"I volunteered to bring a salad for the luncheon following my nephew's high school graduation. Since his parents live on a farm and plant the best sweet corn in the area, I thought it was appropriate to serve this salad using their produce. It was gone before I even had a chance to eat—and I tripled the recipe!"

SALAD

4 ears corn, shucked, or 2 cups frozen whole kernel corn, thawed

1 tablespoon extra virgin olive oil

1 jalapeño chile, seeded and finely chopped

One 15-ounce can black beans, rinsed and drained

1 large red bell pepper, cut into 1-inch pieces

1 cup cherry tomatoes, halved

4 green onions, cut on the diagonal into ½-inch pieces (green parts only)

½ cup chopped red onions

DRESSING

¾ cup bottled reduced-calorie Italian salad dressing

2 tablespoons chopped cilantro or parsley

2 tablespoons lime juice

1 garlic clove, minced

½ teaspoon ground cumin

½ teaspoon Tabasco sauce

¾ teaspoon salt

1. To prepare the salad, cut the kernels off the ears of corn. Heat the olive oil in a large skillet over medium-high heat. Add the corn and jalapeño. Cook until the corn is lightly browned, 2 to 3 minutes, stirring frequently. Transfer to a large bowl; cool slightly. Stir in the black beans, bell pepper, tomatoes, and green and red onions.

2. To prepare the dressing, combine the bottled dressing, cilantro, lime juice, garlic, cumin, Tabasco, and salt in a jar. Secure the lid and shake vigorously to thoroughly blend. Pour all of the dressing over the corn mixture, cover with plastic wrap, and refrigerate for at least 6 hours or overnight.

3. To serve, toss lightly and transfer to a salad bowl lined with lettuce leaves, if desired.

Creamy Kidney Bean Salad

Marilee Mersereau, Manteno, Illinois

Serves 8

"I love to cook and created this recipe after my husband and I had a similar salad while dining at a restaurant. I've served it at many birthday parties, picnics, and family get-togethers."

1. Combine the sour cream, mayonnaise, ketchup, sugar, salt, pepper, and Tabasco in a medium bowl; mix until smooth.

2. Add the kidney beans, green onions, and celery; stir until blended. Cover with plastic wrap and refrigerate for 4 hours to allow the flavors to blend.

½ cup sour cream

⅓ cup mayonnaise

¼ cup ketchup

3 tablespoons sugar

½ teaspoon salt

¼ teaspoon black pepper

½ teaspoon Tabasco sauce

Two 15-ounce cans red kidney beans, rinsed and drained

1 cup finely chopped green onions (green parts only)

2 medium celery stalks, chopped

Easy Coleslaw

Waneta Stephens, Mount Pulaski, Illinois

Serves 8

"*I* have never taken this slaw anywhere that someone didn't want the recipe. The crowning glory was when the VFW asked me to make it for their ham and bean supper. My husband cut the cabbage and I made the dressing for two hundred servings. People bought the slaw that was left over!"

DRESSING

1 cup sugar

½ cup white vinegar

1 teaspoon prepared mustard

SLAW

4 cups chopped cabbage

4 medium celery stalks, sliced

1 medium red bell pepper, chopped

½ medium green bell pepper, chopped

2 tablespoons salt

1. To prepare the dressing, combine the sugar, white vinegar, and the prepared mustard in a medium saucepan. Add ½ cup water and cook over medium-high heat until the sugar and mustard are dissolved. Remove from the heat and let stand for 1 hour.

2. To prepare the slaw, combine the cabbage, celery, bell peppers, salt, and 2 cups ice water in a large bowl; mix well. Cover with plastic wrap and refrigerate for 1 hour.

3. Drain the slaw mixture, squeezing out any excess liquid. Return to the bowl and add the dressing. Cover with plastic wrap and refrigerate for at least 2 hours before serving. The slaw will keep in the refrigerator for 6 to 8 weeks in an airtight container.

Buttermilk Coleslaw

Mary Jaskolka, Hot Springs, Arkansas

Serves 8

"I'm from New Orleans, a Hurricane Katrina evacuee, now living in Arkansas. My new neighbors at the apartment complex here in Hot Springs love this slaw."

1. Combine the raisins, orange juice, lemon juice, and sugar in a large bowl; stir to blend. Let stand for 5 minutes to slightly soften the raisins.

2. Add the buttermilk and mayonnaise and stir with a fork until well blended. Add the coleslaw mix and toss until well blended. Cover with plastic wrap and refrigerate for 2 hours before serving. Season with salt and pepper.

1 cup raisins

¼ cup orange juice

3 tablespoons fresh lemon juice

1 to 2 tablespoons sugar or pourable sugar substitute, such as Splenda

1 cup buttermilk

½ cup mayonnaise

One 16-ounce package shredded coleslaw mix

Salt and pepper

TIPS FROM OUR TEST KITCHEN: This light-on-the-sugar, light-on-the-mayo coleslaw is a refreshing version of a very familiar favorite.

Cranberry Walnut Cabbage Slaw

Linda Bier, Hannibal, Missouri

Serves 10 to 12

"*O*ur Church Hill Circle gets together once a month to sew quilts for our families, friends, and charities. I have shared this recipe with this group as well as at church and family gatherings."

½ cup mayonnaise

2 tablespoons sweet pickle relish

2 tablespoons honey mustard

2 tablespoons honey

½ teaspoon ground white pepper

¼ teaspoon celery seeds

One 16-ounce package shredded
    coleslaw mix

⅔ cup chopped walnuts

1 celery stalk, finely chopped

1 medium onion, finely chopped

½ medium red bell pepper, finely
    chopped

1 cup dried cranberries

1. Combine the mayonnaise, relish, mustard, honey, white pepper, and celery seeds in a medium bowl; stir until well blended.

2. Combine the slaw mix, walnuts, celery, onion, bell pepper, and cranberries in a large bowl. Add the dressing mixture, and toss gently to coat thoroughly. Cover with plastic wrap and refrigerate for 2 hours or up to 6 hours for peak flavors and texture.

TIPS FROM OUR TEST KITCHEN: This tastes like a coleslaw version of a Waldorf salad.

Joy's Potato Salad

Ann Langenfeld, Burns, Oregon

Serves 10 to 12

"This is a family favorite. My mother-in-law, Joy, makes this salad at almost every family gathering during the summer. My husband loves it."

1. To prepare the salad, place the potatoes in a large pot, cover with water, and boil until just tender. Drain well and return to the hot pot for 2 to 3 minutes so that excess water will evaporate. Remove the potatoes to a large bowl and add the onion, eggs, pickles, and black olives.

2. To prepare the dressing, combine the mayonnaise, mustard, pickle juice, salt, and pepper in a small bowl; whisk until smooth. Pour the dressing over the potato mixture; toss gently to mix.

3. Spoon into a 13×9-inch dish and refrigerate at least 2 hours before serving.

SALAD

6 to 8 large potatoes (about 3 pounds), peeled and cut into bite-size pieces

1 medium onion, finely chopped

6 to 8 hard-cooked eggs, peeled and chopped

3 large dill pickles, diced, or ¾ cup dill pickle relish

One 2-ounce can sliced black olives, drained, optional

DRESSING

1½ cups mayonnaise

2 to 3 tablespoons prepared mustard

2 tablespoons dill pickle juice or cider vinegar

1½ teaspoons salt

½ teaspoon black pepper

TIPS FROM OUR TEST KITCHEN: Placing the potato salad in a shallow pan allows the mixture to cool more quickly and evenly.

Strawberry Nut Salad

Vickie Smith, Warsaw, Missouri

Serves 12 to 15

"This dish has a great combination of tastes. I take it to church luncheons and work parties, where everyone asks for the recipe. It also makes a great summertime picnic dish. Serve it from the baking dish or slice into squares and place them on lettuce leaves."

Two 3-ounce packages strawberry gelatin

Two 10-ounce packages frozen sweetened strawberries, thawed

One 8-ounce can crushed pineapple in heavy syrup, drained

3 medium bananas, mashed

1 cup pecan pieces, toasted, if desired

2 cups sour cream

1. Soak the gelatin in ½ cup cold water in a large bowl for 3 to 5 minutes. Stir in 1 cup boiling water. Gently stir in the strawberries, pineapple, bananas, and pecans.

2. Pour half of the gelatin mixture into a 13×9-inch baking dish. Refrigerate the dish until the mixture is slightly thickened, about 1 hour. Keep the remaining gelatin mixture at room temperature.

3. Spread the sour cream carefully over the jelled mixture. Spoon the remaining gelatin mixture on top of the sour cream layer. Cover with plastic wrap and refrigerate for at least 4 hours to overnight before serving.

Strawberry Orange Salad with Glazed Almonds

Patsy Zant, Lamesa, Texas

"This is my own recipe, and at family gatherings and reunions, this salad is always the first food to go. Everyone loves it. It has become our family's favorite food."

1. Preheat the oven to 325°F.

2. To prepare the almonds, pour the butter into a 9-inch-square baking pan. Combine the egg white and sugar in a small bowl and beat with a whisk until frothy. Stir in the almonds and coat well. Pour into the prepared pan.

3. Bake for 20 minutes, stirring every 5 minutes. Remove to wax paper to cool. When the almonds are cool, break apart.

4. To prepare the dressing, combine the sugar, poppy seeds, mustard, and salt in a bowl and beat with a mixer at low speed. Add the vinegar and onion juice and beat at medium speed for 3 minutes. Gradually add the oil in a steady stream until the mixture is thick. Pour into a jar and secure the lid tightly. Refrigerate until 30 minutes before serving time. Remove the dressing from the refrigerator and let come to room temperature.

ALMONDS

2 tablespoons butter, melted

1 egg white

¼ cup sugar

1 cup sliced raw almonds

DRESSING

¾ cup sugar

1½ tablespoons poppy seeds

1 teaspoon dry mustard

1 teaspoon salt

⅓ cup cider vinegar

1½ teaspoons onion juice or
**   2 teaspoons grated onion**

1 cup vegetable or canola oil

SALAD

One 9-ounce package romaine lettuce,
**   torn into bite-size pieces**

2 to 3 cups baby spinach leaves

One 11-ounce can mandarin oranges,
**   drained**

continued

20 strawberries, cut in half

6 green onions, chopped (white and green parts)

5. To prepare the salad, combine the romaine lettuce, spinach, oranges, strawberries, and green onions in a large bowl. Add the glazed almonds. Shake the dressing in the jar to blend; pour over the salad. Toss gently. Serve immediately.

TIPS FROM OUR TEST KITCHEN: Onion juice is found in the spice section at the grocery store. Don't skip glazing the almonds. That's what makes the salad spectacular. Store leftover glazed almonds in the freezer.

Chicken Salad

Julia Webster, Cadiz, Kentucky

Serves 8

"*T*his salad is great to take to any gathering. It can be served as a sandwich, with crackers, on a lettuce leaf, or in a wrap with shredded lettuce and chopped tomatoes."

1. Place the chicken in a Dutch oven. Add enough water to just cover the chicken. Bring to a boil; reduce the heat, and simmer, uncovered, for 12 to 15 minutes, until the chicken is no longer pink in the center. Drain well, cool, and shred. Do not chop.

2. Combine the chicken, thyme, salt, and pepper in a large bowl; mix well. Add the salad dressing and toss to coat completely. Add the celery, grapes, and almonds; toss to mix well. Add the sugar for a sweeter flavor, if using.

8 boneless, skinless chicken breasts
  (about 6 ounces each)
1 tablespoon dried thyme
1 teaspoon salt
½ teaspoon black pepper
1½ to 1¾ cups salad dressing or
  mayonnaise
3 to 4 medium celery stalks, thinly
  sliced
2 cups seedless grapes, cut in half
2 cups sliced almonds, lightly toasted, if
  desired
2 to 3 tablespoons sugar, optional

Lebanese Summer Salad

Vicki Wilder, Englewood, Florida

Serves 6

"*I*n order to make this recipe perfect you must have 'tasters' while preparing the dish. My tasters are my family members who determine what to add—more salt, oil, lemon, or whatever. What fun!"

½ cup bulgur wheat

6 medium tomatoes, seeded and finely chopped (1½ pounds)

1 bunch green onions, finely chopped (white and green parts)

1 bunch parsley, finely chopped

2 tablespoons finely chopped mint leaves

½ cup vegetable, canola, or extra virgin olive oil

Juice of 2 lemons (¼ cup)

2 teaspoons salt, or to taste

Combine the bulgur wheat and ½ cup cold water in a medium bowl. Let stand for 40 minutes, or until the liquid is absorbed. Add the remaining ingredients, stir to blend, cover with plastic wrap, and refrigerate overnight.

TIPS FROM OUR TEST KITCHEN: It's very important to allow the bulgur mixture to chill overnight in order for the bulgur to soften and absorb the other flavors.

Pasta Pizza Salad

Gloria Stevens, Kingsville, Ohio

Serves 12

*"T*his is a pasta salad recipe I have prepared for many potluck dinners at our church and at work and for many family reunion picnics. We live on Lake Erie and do a lot of fishing. This is a great salad to go with most all of my Lake Erie perch and walleye recipes."

1. Cook the shell macaroni according to the package directions. Drain the pasta in a colander and run under cold water to cool quickly. Drain well.

2. Combine the macaroni, tomatoes, mozzarella, onion, olive oil, vinegar, oregano, salt, pepper, garlic powder, and olives, if using, in a large salad bowl. Toss gently to blend well.

3. Serve immediately, or cover with plastic wrap and refrigerate up to 24 hours. Sprinkle with the Parmesan and croutons at serving time.

8 ounces uncooked shell macaroni

3 medium tomatoes, chopped

1 pound mozzarella, cubed

1 medium red onion, sliced into thin rings

½ cup extra virgin olive oil

¼ cup rice wine vinegar

1 teaspoon dried oregano

1 teaspoon salt

¼ teaspoon black pepper

⅛ teaspoon garlic powder, or to taste

½ cup pitted black olives, cut in half, optional

1 tablespoon grated Parmesan, or to taste

¾ cup Italian herb croutons, or to taste

Shrimp Pasta Salad

Dorothea Ableidinger, New Prague, Minnesota

Serves 6 to 8

"This salad was always a treat for our girls when they came home from college to visit."

One 7-ounce package small pasta shells

One 10-ounce package frozen green peas

10 ounces frozen cooked shrimp, thawed

6 medium radishes, thinly sliced

½ medium green bell pepper, finely chopped

2 tablespoons finely chopped onion

One 2-ounce jar chopped pimientos, drained

½ cup mayonnaise

1 tablespoon prepared horseradish sauce

1 teaspoon seasoned salt, or to taste

1. Cook the pasta according to the package directions. Drain in a colander and run under cold water for 20 seconds; drain well. Combine the pasta, peas, shrimp, radishes, bell pepper, onion, and pimientos in a bowl; mix well.

2. Mix the mayonnaise, horseradish, and seasoned salt in a small bowl. Add to the shrimp mixture and toss gently to coat completely. Cover with plastic wrap and refrigerate at least 4 hours to overnight.

Sweet and Sour Dressing with Mixed Green Salad
Janice Adams, Jefferson, Wisconsin

"Whenever I have to take a dish to a potluck, they want me to bring this dressing. I pour the dressing and French fried onions on a mixed green salad as soon as we are ready to eat."

Combine the onion and vinegar in a blender container. Blend until smooth. Add the dry ingredients and the oil; blend well. Serve over a mixed green salad with lettuce, carrots, green bell pepper, and celery. Top with French fried onions.

1 medium onion

¾ cup cider vinegar

1 teaspoon dry mustard

2 teaspoons salt

1 teaspoon celery seeds

1¾ cups sugar

2 cups vegetable or canola oil

Mixed green salad, including vegetables such as carrots, green bell pepper, and celery

French's Original French Fried Onions

TIPS FROM OUR TEST KITCHEN: For a very simple salad, pour some dressing over sliced cucumbers and let stand for 5 minutes before serving.

Sides

Side dishes are never an aside for families and friends who bring their best contributions to food-laden tables at home and church, and for reunions or other events in their communities.

Often, the recipes are handed down through the generations as daughters, daughters-in-law, and even granddaughters carry on a tradition of cooking a special dish that makes a meal complete. Others come about through adding a twist to a tried-and-true side item.

Karen Crunk of Lorena, Texas, says her husband's grandmother made the best holiday dressing. When Crunk joined the family, she watched and made notes, since there was no written recipe. When she took over hosting the holiday feasts, Crunk set out to recreate the special dressing, and her Old-Fashioned Corn Bread Dressing is the result.

When it's time to celebrate birthdays, holidays, and cattle roundups in the ghost town of Dos Cabeza, Arizona, Cheryl Boutin knows what her contribution will be. Her Homestyle Grits Casserole is always popular among residents of the close-knit neighborhood sixteen miles south of Willcox. This casserole can also be prepared a day ahead and then baked on the day of the event.

With sharp Cheddar and Tabasco to give it extra punch, Sheryl Crumpton's Baked Macaroni and Cheese never fails to please. Crumpton, of Lindale, Texas, says the casserole gets rave reviews with its creamy flavor and crunch on top. The one down side to the dish? Crumpton says once you get a taste of it, "Be prepared to overeat!"

For Anthony Massaro of Monroeville, Pennsylvania, honoring his southern Italian heritage comes naturally when he prepares Spaghetti Mezzogirono. The pasta is a classic from his mother and was a staple on the family's holiday table. Massaro says the simple peasant pasta goes well with hearty, crusty bread.

Pamela Shank of Parkersburg, West Virginia, also looks to her mother for inspiration for her Old-Fashioned Scalloped Potatoes. Shank says her mother made everything from scratch but never used a recipe or wrote down her own. Working from memory and experiments, Shank came up with her own rich, delicious version of the potato classic.

In Columbia City, Oregon, the heat can range from mild to hot in Kathy Keudell's popular Dish of Fire, with rice, cheese, chiles, and Tabasco. Keudell, who has perfected the dish over a quarter century, says she never brings home any leftovers and often shares the recipe.

Homesteaders' Four-Bean Casserole

Betty Cochran, West Danville, Vermont

Serves 10 to 12

"I've made this recipe for many years for community gatherings, church suppers, and family get-togethers. Everyone loves it!"

1. Cook the bacon in a large skillet over medium-high heat until crisp. Remove the bacon and drain on paper towels; crumble and set aside. Add the onions, syrup, garlic powder, and dry mustard to the pan drippings. Reduce the heat to medium and add the vinegar slowly, taking care because hot steam will rise. Cover and cook for 20 minutes.

2. Preheat the oven to 350°F. Grease a 3-quart casserole or 13×9-inch baking dish. Add the beans to the pan. Stir in the onion mixture and the crumbled bacon; mix well.

3. Cover and bake for 45 minutes. Remove from the oven, uncover, and let stand for 20 to 25 minutes before serving.

8 bacon slices

3 to 4 medium onions, cut into rings and separated

½ to ¾ cup maple syrup or packed dark brown sugar

1½ teaspoons garlic powder

1 teaspoon dry mustard

¼ cup cider vinegar

One 15-ounce can dark red kidney beans, drained

One 15-ounce can lima beans, drained

One 16-ounce can butter beans, drained

One 16-ounce can baked beans, undrained

TIPS FROM OUR TEST KITCHEN: The onion mixture will harden when added to the beans, but will break down during the baking process.

Bell Peppers with Peanuts and Water Chestnuts

Tammi Kaiser, Glenview, Illinois

Serves 4 to 6

"This is a quick and easy side dish to take anywhere. It is very easy to heat up as well."

3 tablespoons reduced-sodium soy sauce

1 tablespoon hoisin sauce

3 tablespoons peanut oil

1 medium yellow bell pepper, cut into
   ¼-inch slices

1 medium green bell pepper, cut into
   ¼-inch slices

1 medium red bell pepper, cut into
   ¼-inch slices

One 8-ounce can sliced water chestnuts,
   drained

½ cup unsalted peanuts

2 garlic cloves, minced

1. Combine the soy sauce and hoisin sauce in a small bowl. Heat the peanut oil in a large skillet or wok over high heat. Add the bell peppers and cook until just tender, about 4 minutes, stirring constantly. Use two utensils for easy stirring.

2. Add the water chestnuts, peanuts, and garlic. Cook for 1 minute, stirring constantly. Serve immediately for peak flavors and texture.

TIPS FROM OUR TEST KITCHEN: Hoisin sauce is sold in the international foods section of major supermarkets.

Broccoli Elegant

Linda Shires, Caldwell, West Virginia

Serves 6 to 8

"*A* friend shared this recipe with me over twenty years ago. It is a favorite of my family. We use it often during the Thanksgiving holiday, Christmas season, and for family picnics and reunions."

1. Preheat the oven to 350°F. Grease a 13×9-inch baking dish.

2. Combine 1½ cups water and 4 tablespoons of the butter in a large saucepan. Bring to a boil; remove from the heat. Stir in the stuffing mix and let stand for 5 minutes.

3. Spoon the stuffing around the edge of the prepared pan, leaving a well in the center. Arrange the broccoli spears in the well.

4. Melt the remaining 2 tablespoons butter in a saucepan over medium-low heat. Add the flour, stirring until smooth. Cook for 1 minute, stirring constantly. Add the bouillon.

5. Add the milk gradually and cook over medium heat for 3 minutes, or until thickened, stirring constantly. Whisk in the cream cheese and the salt, mixing until smooth. Stir in the onion. Pour the sauce over the broccoli. Sprinkle with the Cheddar and paprika.

6. Cover with foil and bake for 35 minutes. Remove the foil and bake for 10 minutes longer.

6 tablespoons butter or margarine

One 6-ounce package chicken-flavored stuffing mix

Two 10-ounce packages frozen broccoli spears, thawed and drained

2 teaspoons all-purpose flour

1 teaspoon chicken bouillon granules

¾ cup milk

One 3-ounce package cream cheese, softened

¼ teaspoon salt

1 medium onion, finely chopped

1 cup shredded Cheddar

Paprika

Calico Cabbage

Josie Lakin, Pikeville, Kentucky

"*I* share this recipe at my senior citizens center and with my church family and also serve it for special dinners in my home."

1 small head cabbage, cut into 1-inch
    wedges
2 large carrots, julienned
2 medium celery stalks, julienned
1 large onion, quartered
2 to 3 tablespoons sugar
1 teaspoon salt, or to taste
1/8 to 1/4 teaspoon black pepper
1/2 cup (1 stick) butter or margarine, cut
    into small pieces

1. Preheat the oven to 350°F. Grease a 13×9-inch baking pan.

2. Combine the cabbage, carrots, celery, and onion in the prepared pan. Sprinkle the sugar, salt, and pepper over the top. Dot with butter.

3. Cover with foil and bake for 30 minutes. Uncover and stir the mixture. Recover and bake for 25 to 30 minutes longer, until the cabbage and carrots are tender. Season with additional salt, if desired.

Haluski
(Cabbage and Noodles)

Marianne Ozmina, Warrior Run, Pennsylvania

"My husband's aunt taught me how to make Haluski. It's really delicious."

1. Heat a Dutch oven over medium heat. Add the bacon and onion, and cook until the onion begins to brown, and the bacon is almost cooked, stirring frequently. Add the cabbage, stir until well coated, and cook for 30 minutes over low heat, stirring occasionally.

2. Add the sauerkraut, butter, ⅔ cup water, the caraway seeds, and sugar. Mix well and cook, uncovered, over low heat for 1 hour, or until the cabbage is very tender, stirring occasionally.

3. Cook the noodles according to the package directions. Drain and add to the cabbage mixture; mix well. Season with salt and pepper.

1 pound bacon, chopped

1 large onion, chopped

1 head cabbage (1 to 1½ pounds), shredded

One 14-ounce can sauerkraut, well rinsed and drained

½ cup (1 stick) butter or margarine

1 teaspoon caraway seeds

1 teaspoon sugar

6 to 8 ounces uncooked wide egg noodles

Salt and pepper

TIPS FROM OUR TEST KITCHEN: Before adding the noodles, set aside some of the cabbage mixture for use on hot dogs, if desired. For ease in chopping the bacon, place in the freezer for 1 hour before cutting.

Company's Coming Corn Casserole
Margee Berry, Trout Lake, Washington

"*I* created this recipe for Easter brunch, and everyone loved it because of the cheesy, spicy flavor. I ended up serving it again for a New Year's Day open house since it really can be served anytime. It is easy to put together the day before, just cover and refrigerate. Then, just before the party, finish it by baking."

2 tablespoons extra virgin olive oil

1 large onion, chopped

1½ cups frozen corn kernels, thawed

½ medium red bell pepper, chopped

6 medium garlic cloves, minced

½ teaspoon ground cumin

½ teaspoon chili powder

4 eggs

One 10-ounce can red enchilada sauce

One 4-ounce can chopped green chiles, undrained

4 cups 1-inch French bread cubes

One 8-ounce package shredded Mexican cheese blend

3 medium green onions, chopped (white and green parts)

1. Preheat the oven to 350°F. Grease an 11×7-inch baking dish.

2. Heat the olive oil in a large skillet over medium heat. Add the onion, corn, and bell pepper. Cook until the onion begins to brown, about 15 minutes, stirring frequently. Add the garlic, cumin, and chili powder and cook until very fragrant, about 1 minute, stirring constantly.

3. Whisk the eggs and enchilada sauce in a large bowl. Fold in the chiles, bread cubes, and 1 cup of the cheese. Stir in the corn mixture. Pour into the prepared pan. Sprinkle evenly with the green onions.

4. Bake, uncovered, for 45 minutes, or until golden and a knife inserted in the center comes out clean. Top with the remaining cheese and let stand for 5 minutes before serving.

Cheesy Slow Cooker Corn

Donna Richards, Tucson, Arizona

Serves 12 to 16

"I get lots of requests to bring this yummy dish to potlucks. I love to bring this corn because it's so easy and it goes over so well."

Combine the corn, American cheese, butter, milk, sugar, and 3 tablespoons water in a greased 4- to 5-quart slow cooker. Mix well. Cover and cook on low for 3 to 4 hours, until the corn is thoroughly heated and the cheese is melted. Stir in the cream cheese and heat until melted. Season with salt and pepper.

Three 16-ounce packages frozen corn kernels

6 slices American cheese, torn into small pieces

¼ cup (½ stick) butter, cut into small pieces

3 tablespoons milk

2 tablespoons sugar

11 to 12 ounces cream cheese, cut into small pieces and softened

Salt and pepper

Old-Fashioned Corn Bread Dressing

Karen Crunk, Lorena, Texas

"So many times I have heard women say, 'I'll prepare the holiday meal, but I don't know how to make dressing.' My husband's grandmother made the best but never used a recipe. I watched her a few times to get the basics. When she passed away, it became my job to host the holiday meals, so I did the best I could and jotted down what I remembered. I think his grandmother would approve."

**Two 6-ounce packages yellow corn
    bread mix**
1⅓ cups milk
1 medium celery stalk, chopped
½ cup (1 stick) butter or margarine
1 medium onion, chopped
7 slices day-old white bread
2 eggs, beaten
2 hard-cooked eggs, chopped
Three 14-ounce cans chicken broth
1 teaspoon poultry seasoning
1 teaspoon salt
1 teaspoon black pepper
Chopped, cooked giblets, optional

1. Combine the corn bread mix, milk, and celery in a large bowl; mix well. Bake in a pan according to the package directions. Remove to a wire rack to cool completely.

2. Melt the butter in a medium skillet over medium heat. Add the onion and cook until tender, about 7 minutes, stirring frequently.

3. Preheat the oven to 325°F. Grease a 13×9-inch casserole.

4. Crumble the cooled corn bread and day-old white bread into a large mixing bowl. Add the onion, beaten eggs, hard-cooked eggs, broth, poultry seasoning, salt, pepper, and giblets, if using. Spoon into the prepared dish.

5. Bake, uncovered, for 55 minutes, or until lightly golden and a knife inserted in the center comes out clean.

Slow Cooker Dressing

Jan Mayland, Shepherd, Montana

Serves 12

"I have made this recipe for years at Thanksgiving and Christmas meals, as we all love dressing."

1. Melt the butter in a large skillet over medium heat. Add the onions, celery, and mushrooms. Cook until the onions are translucent, about 12 minutes, stirring frequently.

2. Place the bread cubes in a large bowl, add the onion mixture, and mix well. Combine the eggs and broth in another bowl. Combine the remaining ingredients in another bowl and add to the egg mixture. Mix well and add to the bowl with bread cubes.

3. Spoon the mixture into a greased 3- to 4-quart slow cooker. Cover and cook on high for 45 minutes. Reduce the heat to low and cook for 4 hours longer.

1 cup (2 sticks) butter or margarine

3 medium onions, chopped

4 medium celery stalks, chopped

One 13-ounce can sliced mushrooms, drained

12 cups dried ½-inch bread cubes (15 to 16 bread slices)

2 eggs, well beaten

3 cups chicken or turkey broth

1 teaspoon poultry seasoning

½ to 1 teaspoon salt

1 to 1½ teaspoons rubbed sage

1 teaspoon dried thyme

¼ to ½ teaspoon black pepper

Chopped cooked giblets, optional

TIPS FROM OUR TEST KITCHEN: To dry bread cubes, place on two large baking sheets; cover with clean dishtowels and let stand overnight. You also may bake the bread cubes in a preheated 350°F oven for 5 minutes. Cool for 5 minutes.

Homestyle Grits Casserole

Cheryl Boutin, Willcox, Arizona

Serves 12 to 16

"*E*ven though our address is Willcox, we really live in Dos Cabeza—a ghost town sixteen miles south of Willcox. Dos Cabeza is a tight-knit little neighborhood, and parties take place for birthdays, holidays, roundups (when the cattle are brought down from the mountains), and just because we like to get together. I am often asked to make this casserole."

1½ cups regular grits

1 teaspoon salt

4 cups shredded Cheddar

3 eggs, well beaten

¾ cup (1½ sticks) butter

1½ teaspoons garlic salt or onion salt

Dash of Tabasco sauce

One 4-ounce can chopped green chiles, optional

One 2-ounce can French's Original French Fried Onions, crushed

1. Preheat the oven to 350°F. Grease a 13×9-inch baking pan.

2. Bring 6 cups water to a boil in a large saucepan. Add the grits and salt and return to a boil. Reduce the heat to medium and cook, uncovered, for 5 minutes, or until thickened. Remove from the heat.

3. Add the cheese, eggs, butter, garlic salt, Tabasco, and chiles, if using; mix well. Pour into the prepared pan. Bake for 50 minutes. Sprinkle the crushed onions on top and bake for 10 minutes longer.

TIPS FROM OUR TEST KITCHEN: The grits casserole may be prepared a day ahead and refrigerated until baking time.

Baked Macaroni and Cheese

Sheryl Crumpton, Lindale, Texas

Serves 12 to 16

"I have taken this macaroni dish to church potlucks and to family or friend get-togethers and have served it at home. It always gets rave reviews. It's creamy, yet a little crunchy on top. Just get ready to overeat when you taste this. It's a favorite for all ages."

1. Preheat the oven to 350°F. Grease a 13×9-inch baking pan.

2. Bring 6 cups water and 3 teaspoons of the salt to a boil in a large saucepan. Slowly stir in the macaroni. Return to a boil and cook for 9 to 11 minutes, stirring occasionally. The macaroni should be tender but firm. Drain in a colander and rinse briefly with cold water. Drain well, shaking off any excess liquid. Off the heat, toss the macaroni with the butter in the same saucepan; set aside.

3. Beat the eggs in a medium bowl until light yellow. Add the evaporated milk, the remaining 1 teaspoon salt, and the Tabasco. Combine the Cheddar and American cheese in a small bowl.

4. Place half of the macaroni in the prepared pan. Sprinkle half of the cheese mixture evenly over the top. Place the remaining macaroni on top and add the remaining cheese. Slowly pour the egg mixture over the macaroni mixture and spread evenly over the top. Sprinkle with the paprika.

5. Cover and bake for 20 minutes, then uncover and bake for 20 minutes longer, or until the custard is set and the top is bubbly and golden brown.

4 teaspoons salt

8 ounces uncooked elbow macaroni

6 tablespoons butter, softened

2 eggs

2 cups evaporated milk

2 to 3 dashes Tabasco sauce, or to taste

4 cups shredded extra-sharp Cheddar

2 ounces American cheese (about 3 slices), shredded or torn into small pieces

½ teaspoon paprika

TIPS FROM OUR TEST KITCHEN: Be sure to cover the casserole for the first 20 minutes or the top will get too brown.

Spaghetti Mezzogirono

Anthony G. Massaro, Monroeville, Pennsylvania

Serves 6

"*T*his pasta recipe comes from an old southern Italian classic from my mother. It is a simple peasant pasta to be eaten with a hearty, crusty bread. Growing up in my family, we had this pasta only on holidays. On Christmas Eve, it was served with one small can of anchovies. Traditionally, seven different fishes are presented on Christmas Eve, ensuring good luck, health, and harmony in the New Year."

8 ounces uncooked spaghetti, broken in
    half
¼ cup olive oil
1 medium green bell pepper, cut into
    very thin strips
1 medium red bell pepper, cut into very
    thin strips
5 garlic cloves, minced
One 2-ounce can anchovies, optional
¼ cup chopped parsley
½ cup white wine (Muscat, Savignon
    Blanc, or Chenin Blanc)
Grated Romano or Parmesan

1. Cook the pasta according to the package directions until al dente. Drain and place in a pasta bowl.

2. To prepare the sauce, heat the olive oil in a large skillet over medium heat. Add the bell peppers and cook until very tender, about 15 minutes. Add the garlic and anchovies, if using, and cook for 30 seconds. Add the parsley and wine; remove from the heat.

3. Spoon ¾ cup of the sauce over the pasta and toss to blend. Place the remaining sauce in a bowl to pass at the table with the cheese.

TIPS FROM OUR TEST KITCHEN: For a thinner sauce, reserve ½ cup of the pasta cooking liquid and add with the wine.

Pineapple Casserole

Rachel Henderson, The Villages, Florida

Serves 8

"*T*his Pineapple Casserole goes well with ham or chicken. It is my most-asked-for dish."

1. Preheat the oven to 350°F. Grease a 13×9-inch baking pan.

2. Drain the pineapple, reserving ½ cup of the juice. Arrange the chunks in the bottom of the prepared pan.

3. Combine the reserved juice, flour, and sugar in a mixing bowl. Whisk until smooth and pour evenly over the pineapple. Sprinkle with the Cheddar cheese and cracker crumbs and dot with the butter.

4. Bake for 35 minutes, or until golden brown.

Two 20-ounce cans pineapple chunks, drained, ½ cup juice reserved

⅓ cup self-rising flour

⅔ cup sugar or pourable sugar substitute, such as Splenda

2 cups (8 ounces) shredded sharp Cheddar

1 sleeve butter crackers, crushed

½ cup (1 stick) cold butter, cut into small pieces

Best-Ever Fried Potatoes

Liz Donath, Philadelphia, Missouri

Serves 4 to 5

"*T*his is usually served on a day when we fry up a mess of fresh catfish the men have caught fishing on the river near our farm here in Missouri. I made this recipe up years ago, and it is always well liked. We usually have it on the Fourth of July."

¼ cup vegetable oil, olive oil, or vegetable shortening

2 tablespoons butter

1½ pounds red potatoes, peeled, if desired, and sliced

½ medium green bell pepper, chopped

½ cup French's Original French Fried Onions

¼ cup bacon bits

¼ teaspoon salt

⅛ teaspoon black pepper

¼ teaspoon garlic powder

1. Heat the oil and butter in a large skillet over medium-high heat.

2. Combine the potatoes with the remaining ingredients in a large bowl. When the oil is hot, add the potato mixture and cook until the potatoes are tender, about 12 minutes. Stir frequently using two utensils, as for a stir-fry, for easy handling. Adjust the seasonings if needed.

3. Remove from the heat and let stand for 5 minutes before serving.

TIPS FROM OUR TEST KITCHEN: This recipe may be doubled easily, but use two large skillets for even cooking.

Nanny Gawne's Potato and Onion Pancakes

Robert Gawne, Waymart, Pennsylvania

"*F*or over forty-five years, thousands have enjoyed this recipe at our summer church fund raiser. Once you've had them, you'll want more."

1. Arrange the potatoes on the bottom of a stockpot. Top with the onions. Add enough water to cover, about 2½ quarts. Bring to a boil and cook until the potatoes are tender and the onions are soft, but slightly firm, about 13 minutes. If necessary, remove the potatoes and continue cooking the onions for 5 to 10 minutes longer.

2. Remove from the heat and cool the onions slightly. Remove the outer skins and place the onions in a large mixing bowl. Spoon the potatoes on top of the onions and sprinkle with the salt and pepper. Reserve the cooking liquid. Let stand for 10 to 15 minutes.

3. Preheat the oven to 200°F.

4. Beat the potato mixture with a mixer at low speed. Gradually increase the speed to medium and beat in the eggs one at a time. Add the flour and mix until the mixture forms a thick batter. Add a small amount of the cooking liquid if the mixture appears dry. Fold in the French fried onions.

5. With floured hands, form the batter into 3-inch rounds. Melt ¼ cup of the shortening in a large skillet or griddle over medium heat. Working in batches, fry the cakes until golden brown on both sides. Place the cooked cakes in the oven to keep warm.

2½ **pounds new potatoes**
2½ **pounds Vidalia onions, cut in half, skins left on**
1 **teaspoon salt**
1 **teaspoon black pepper**
4 **eggs**
1 **cup all-purpose flour**
Two 2-ounce cans French's Original French Fried Onions
1 **cup shortening or lard for frying**

TIPS FROM OUR TEST KITCHEN: To prevent burning hands when peeling the onions, use a clean dishtowel to hold them.

Old-Fashioned Scalloped Potatoes

Pamela Shank, Parkersburg, West Virginia

Serves 12 to 16

"I grew up with a mom who was the greatest cook ever. She made everything from scratch, so scalloped potatoes were always homemade. She never used recipes or wrote anything down, so I try to re-create dishes from memories and experiments. These potatoes are very rich and delicious."

5 pounds baking potatoes, peeled
¼ cup (½ stick) butter
¼ cup all-purpose flour
2 cups heavy cream
2 cups whole milk
8 ounces processed cheese, such as
    Velveeta, cubed
1 teaspoon salt, or to taste
½ teaspoon black pepper, or to taste
2 medium onions, finely chopped
2 cups shredded Cheddar
½ cup grated Parmesan

1. Preheat the oven to 350°F. Coat a 13×9-inch baking pan with nonstick cooking spray.

2. Cut the potatoes into thin slices. Place in a bowl of cold water. Melt the butter in a large saucepan over medium heat. Gradually stir in the flour and cook for 1 minute. Add the heavy cream and milk slowly, stirring constantly. Reduce the heat to low, stir in the processed cheese, salt, and pepper. Cook until the cheese melts, stirring constantly. Remove from the heat.

3. Drain the potatoes well and arrange one-third of them in the prepared pan. Season with additional salt and pepper if desired. Top with one-third of the onions and one-third of the Cheddar. Pour one-third of the cheese sauce over all. Repeat the layers twice.

4. Coat a sheet of aluminum foil with nonstick cooking spray. Tent the foil with the sprayed side down over the casserole. Place on a foil-lined oven rack. Bake for 1½ hours.

5. Remove the foil, sprinkle with the Parmesan, and bake for 20 to 30 minutes longer, until the potatoes are tender.

Premier Hot Potato Salad

Clara Hauck, Richardton, North Dakota

"We served this dish at our daughter's wedding for five hundred with baked ham, hot celery seed rolls, and pickled crab apples. It was a hit and so delicious!"

1. Place the potatoes in a stockpot. Add water to cover. Bring to a boil, reduce the heat, and simmer, uncovered, until the potatoes are just tender when pierced with a fork, about 20 minutes. Do not overcook. Drain and cool on a wire rack for 20 minutes. Peel and slice the potatoes.

2. Preheat the oven to 350°F. Grease a 2-quart baking dish or 12×8-inch baking dish.

3. Combine the soup, sour cream, onion, 2 tablespoons of the parsley, the salt, and pepper in a large bowl; mix well. Add the potatoes, 1 cup of the Cheddar, and the eggs. Toss gently. Spoon the mixture into the prepared pan.

4. Sprinkle the remaining 1½ cups Cheddar over the top, followed by the remaining 2 tablespoons chopped parsley. Coat a sheet of aluminum foil with nonstick cooking spray and cover the casserole, sprayed side down.

5. Bake for 45 minutes, or until the potatoes are thoroughly heated and the cheese melts. Do not overbake.

6 medium potatoes

One 10-ounce can of cream of mushroom soup

1 cup sour cream

1 tablespoon finely chopped onion

¼ cup chopped parsley

1 tablespoon salt

¼ teaspoon black pepper

2½ cups shredded sharp Cheddar

5 hard-cooked eggs, sliced

Ranch Potatoes

Jennifer Langworthy McCormick, Irvine, Kentucky

Serves 6

"Every time we have a family dinner or reunion, my Aunt Frances calls me to ask if I am bringing my potatoes. I never bring any leftovers home!"

4 large baking potatoes

4 ounces cream cheese, softened

¼ cup sour cream

½ medium yellow onion, finely chopped

1 to 2 cups shredded Cheddar, to taste

3 ounces bacon bits

Salt

½ cup milk, scalded

One 1-ounce package dry ranch dressing mix

3 to 4 green onions, finely chopped (white and green parts)

1. Wash and pierce the potatoes in several places with a fork. Microwave on high for 10 minutes until tender. Set aside to cool slightly.

2. Preheat the oven to 350°F. Grease an 11×7-inch baking pan.

3. Combine the cream cheese and sour cream in a large bowl; beat until smooth. Add the yellow onion, half of the Cheddar, and half of the bacon bits. Season with salt. Mix well and set aside.

4. Peel the potatoes when they are cool enough to handle. Add to the cream cheese mixture, using a fork to mix well. Stir in the milk. Add 2 tablespoons of the dry ranch dressing, or more to taste.

5. Spread the potato mixture in the prepared pan. Bake, uncovered, for 30 minutes. Remove from the oven, sprinkle with the remaining Cheddar, the remaining bacon bits, and the green onions. Bake for 5 minutes longer, or until the cheese melts.

Dish of Fire

Kathy Keudell, Columbia City, Oregon

Serves 12 to 16

"*D*ish of Fire is one that gets rave reviews and many requests for the recipe. There are never any leftovers. I've been making it for twenty-four years now. Try it!"

1. Combine the rice, 2 cups water, the bay leaves, and salt in a large saucepan. Bring to a boil, reduce the heat, cover tightly, and simmer for 15 to 20 minutes. Remove from the heat and let stand, covered, 2 to 3 minutes to allow the rice to absorb the liquid. Discard the bay leaves.

2. Preheat the oven to 350°F. Coat a 13×9-inch baking pan with nonstick cooking spray.

3. Melt the butter in a Dutch oven over medium heat. Add the onions and cook until just tender, about 5 minutes, stirring frequently. Add the garlic and cook for 30 seconds. Remove from the heat.

4. Add the rice, sour cream, cottage cheese, Tabasco, cumin, and 3 cups of the shredded cheese to the onions. Stir well.

5. Spoon half of the rice mixture into the prepared pan. Sprinkle with the chiles. Top with the remaining rice mixture, the remaining 1 cup cheese, and the pepper.

6. Bake for 25 to 30 minutes, until bubbly and golden on the edges. Remove from the oven and let stand for 10 minutes before serving.

1 cup uncooked long grain rice, preferably parboiled

2 bay leaves or ½ teaspoon dried oregano

1 teaspoon salt

¼ cup (½ stick) butter or ¼ cup extra virgin olive oil

2 medium onions, chopped

1 garlic clove, minced

2 cups sour cream

1 cup cottage cheese

1 teaspoon Tabasco sauce

1 teaspoon ground cumin

4 cups shredded Monterey Jack, mozzarella, or Mexican-blend cheese

Two 4-ounce cans chopped hot or mild green chiles, drained

¼ teaspoon coarsely ground black pepper

TIPS FROM OUR TEST KITCHEN: This dish can go from mild to wild or somewhere in between. Use hot chiles, mild chiles, or one can of each. Be sure to use chopped chiles, not the pickled variety.

Spanish Rice

Mike Pineda, Carlsbad, New Mexico

Serves 12

"I have used this recipe at family reunions, summer cookouts, and wedding receptions."

⅓ cup vegetable or canola oil

1½ cups uncooked long grain rice

2 medium onions, finely chopped

1 medium green bell pepper, finely chopped

2 medium celery stalks, finely chopped

One 20-ounce can crushed tomatoes, undrained

2 teaspoons ground cumin

2 teaspoons garlic powder

1½ teaspoons salt, or to taste

Two 14-ounce cans chicken broth

1. Heat the oil in a Dutch oven over medium-high heat. Add the rice and cook until golden, about 3 minutes, stirring constantly. Add the onions, bell pepper, celery, tomatoes, cumin, garlic powder, salt, and 1 can of the chicken broth.

2. Bring to a boil, reduce the heat, cover tightly, and simmer for 20 minutes. Add the remaining can of broth; mix well.

Mexican Squash

Esmeralda Maynes, Clayton, New Mexico

Serves 6 to 8

"Serve this squash for get-togethers with friends and family."

Heat the oil in a large skillet over medium-high heat. Add the squash, corn, onion, chiles, and garlic powder. Cook for 12 minutes, or until tender, stirring frequently. Add the butter and salt.

¼ cup canola oil

5 to 6 medium yellow squash or zucchini (about 2 pounds), chopped

4 ears corn, kernels removed, or one 16-ounce can whole kernel corn, drained, or 1½ cups frozen corn kernels

1 medium onion, chopped

4 jalapeño chiles, seeded and chopped

1 tablespoon garlic powder

1 tablespoon butter or margarine

¾ teaspoon salt, or to taste

TIPS FROM OUR TEST KITCHEN: When cooking the vegetables, use two utensils, such as a tablespoon and a fork, to toss and stir as you would a stir-fry. This allows for easier handling and even cooking.

Sweet Potato Casserole

Drichelle Pierce, Albuquerque, New Mexico

Serves 6

"My husband's grandma gave me this recipe after we had been married for a few years. The first time I baked it was for a Christmas potluck. I secretly put the dish on the table with the rest of the food. About five minutes into the dinner, people started asking who had made the casserole. It was a hit! The next week I baked it for my husband's grandma, and she commented on how well I did."

SWEET POTATOES

Two 15-ounce cans sweet potatoes in syrup, drained and mashed

1 cup milk

½ to 1 cup granulated sugar, or to taste

2 eggs

6 tablespoons butter, melted

½ teaspoon ground cinnamon

½ teaspoon ground nutmeg

TOPPING

¾ cup cornflakes

½ cup packed light brown sugar

½ cup chopped pecans or walnuts, toasted, if desired

6 tablespoons butter, melted

1. Preheat the oven to 400°F. Coat an 8-inch-square pan with nonstick cooking spray.

2. To prepare the potatoes, place the drained sweet potatoes in a large bowl. Beat well with a mixer at low speed. Add the milk, granulated sugar, eggs, butter, cinnamon, and nutmeg. Increase the speed to medium and beat until smooth.

3. Spoon into the prepared pan. Bake, uncovered, for 40 minutes, or until a knife inserted in the center comes out clean.

4. To prepare the topping, combine the cornflakes, brown sugar, and pecans in a medium bowl, and stir gently to mix well. Sprinkle evenly over the potato mixture. Drizzle the melted butter evenly over the top. Bake, uncovered, for 25 minutes.

TIPS FROM OUR TEST KITCHEN: For a dish that's less sweet, use 3 pounds of fresh cooked sweet potatoes instead of canned sweet potatoes.

Yamtastic

Ethan Bosch, Clarion, Pennsylvania

Serves 12 to 16

"I've shared this recipe with folks at church after potluck suppers. But Thanksgiving 2005 was the meal where the entire table of relatives agreed that the dish was wonderful—and relatives will tell you the truth!"

1. Preheat the oven to 350°F. Grease a 13×9-inch baking pan.

2. To prepare the potatoes, combine the sweet potatoes, maple syrup, heavy cream, butter, egg, salt, and pepper in a large bowl. Beat until blended with a mixer at low speed. Increase the speed to medium and beat until smooth. Spoon into the prepared pan.

3. To prepare the topping, melt the butter in a medium saucepan over medium-high heat. Remove from the heat and stir in the brown sugar, pecans, and cream. Spread the topping evenly over the sweet potato mixture.

4. Bake, uncovered, for 50 minutes, or until slightly firm on top.

POTATOES

6 pounds sweet potatoes or yams, cooked and peeled

½ cup maple syrup

¼ cup heavy cream

¼ cup (½ stick) butter, softened

1 egg, beaten

½ teaspoon salt

½ teaspoon black pepper

TOPPING

¼ cup (½ stick) butter

¼ cup packed light brown sugar

½ cup chopped pecans

1 tablespoon heavy cream

Green Tomato Casserole

Sylvia L. Bazor, Covington, Tennessee

Serves 4 to 6

"*I*f you like green tomatoes, you will like this recipe. All my friends and family love it!"

4 bread slices, torn into small pieces
   (about 2 cups)
4 medium green tomatoes, cut into
   ¼-inch slices (about 1½ pounds total)
1 teaspoon sugar
1 teaspoon salt
¼ teaspoon black pepper, or to taste
1 cup shredded sharp Cheddar
1 tablespoon butter or margarine

1. Preheat the oven to 400°F. Lightly grease a 1½-quart casserole or deep-dish pie pan.

2. Place the bread in a food processor and pulse to a coarse texture. Arrange half the tomato slices in the bottom of the prepared pan.

3. Combine the sugar, salt, and pepper in a small bowl; mix well. Sprinkle the tomatoes with half the sugar mixture, half the bread crumbs, and ½ cup of the Cheddar. Repeat with a second layer, omitting the Cheddar. Dot the casserole with the butter.

4. Bake, covered, for 1 hour. Uncover and sprinkle the remaining Cheddar on top. Bake for 5 minutes longer, or until the cheese melts. Remove from the oven and let stand for 15 minutes before serving to allow the flavors to blend.

Sun-Dried Tomato Pesto Pasta

Kathy Dicharo, Bryan, Texas

Serves 16

"Where I work we have what we call Food Day about every other month, when everybody brings a dish. Sometimes we have a theme of what type of food to bring. This pasta dish is what I've come up with. It's a simple recipe, with just a few ingredients, but it's big on flavor. I use bowtie pasta because it looks so pretty, but any kind of pasta can be used. This recipe is a favorite for all the workers!"

1. Cook the pasta according to the package directions, drain, and shake off excess water. Meanwhile, cut the tomatoes into julienne strips.

2. Cook the bacon in a large skillet over medium-high heat until crisp. Drain and crumble.

3. Place the pasta in a large bowl. Add the tomatoes and pesto; mix well. Add the bacon and Romano and toss well. For a moister consistency, add some of the reserved sun-dried tomato oil. Season with pepper. Serve immediately.

1 pound uncooked bowtie pasta

One 8-ounce jar sun-dried tomatoes in olive oil, drained, some liquid reserved

8 ounces peppered bacon or bacon with ¼ teaspoon black pepper

One 10-ounce jar basil pesto

1 cup grated Romano

Black pepper

Zucchini Béarnaise

Barbara Guiffre, Herkimer, New York

Serves 6 to 8

"*I* shared this recipe with my colleagues at Herkimer Junior/Senior High School at faculty room luncheon get-togethers before holiday vacations. I just retired from teaching French and Spanish for thirty-two years and am enjoying leisure activities like traveling and cooking. Bon appétit!"

5 medium zucchini, cut into 1-inch
   rounds
3 tablespoons butter
1 small onion, minced
1 tablespoon all-purpose flour
One 10-ounce can cream of golden
   mushroom soup or cream of
   chicken soup
⅔ cup Sauterne or other dry white wine
Salt and pepper
½ cup grated Parmesan
Paprika

1. Preheat the oven to 375°F. Grease an 11×7-inch baking dish.

2. Bring 1 cup water to a boil in a large saucepan. Add the zucchini and return to a boil. Reduce the heat and cook, uncovered, until just tender, about 5 minutes. Drain and cover the bottom of the prepared dish with the zucchini.

3. Melt the butter in the saucepan over medium-low heat. Add the onion and cook for 5 minutes, or until translucent, stirring frequently. Add the flour and mix well. Stir in the soup and wine.

4. Increase the heat to medium-high and bring to a boil, stirring constantly. Boil until the mixture thickens. Season with salt and pepper. Pour the sauce evenly over the zucchini. Sprinkle with the Parmesan and paprika. Bake for 30 minutes, or until bubbly and slightly browned on top.

Zucchini Casserole

Elvira Mileti, Columbia City, Oregon

Serves 8

"*I* first had this casserole at a county fair potluck and thought it was different and delicious. After that, every year that I worked at the Columbia County Fair I would take this dish for the workers' potluck. I have also taken it to numerous other picnics."

1. Preheat the oven to 350°F. Grease a 13×9-inch baking pan.

2. Combine the zucchini, onions, and 1 cup water in a Dutch oven. Bring to a boil, reduce the heat, and simmer, covered, for 5 minutes, or until the zucchini is just tender. Drain in a colander, shaking off any excess liquid.

3. Reserve ½ cup of the stuffing mix. Combine the remaining stuffing mix and the melted butter in a large bowl. Add the zucchini and onions, the carrots, sour cream, and soup; mix well.

4. Spoon the mixture into the prepared pan. Top with the reserved stuffing mix. Bake for 40 to 45 minutes, until golden.

5 medium zucchini (about 2 pounds), thinly sliced

2 medium onions, chopped

One 6-ounce package chicken-flavored stuffing mix

1 cup (2 sticks) butter, melted

1 cup grated carrots

1 cup sour cream

One 10-ounce can cream of chicken soup

Entrées

*A*nytime friends or family get together to enjoy a special meal, the entrée is the star attraction. *American Profile* magazine readers have devised special entrées that fill the bill, no matter what the occasion is.

Karla Myers of Cedar Rapids, Iowa, says Iowans love their casseroles, and when a relative or friend is in need, or a celebration is at hand, she never arrives empty-handed. Her Beef and Noodles is a welcome sight—and Myers says it's her most popular comfort food.

Ever since 1966, when her Beef and Cheese Casserole won first place—and a $6 prize—at the Wheatland, Wyoming, County Fair, Carole Bruere has prepared the dish to the delight of her dinner guests. It is most welcome on chilly nights, Bruere says, and continues to win over family and friends more than forty years after winning the fair prize.

Edgar Galbraith of Jacksonville, North Carolina, has come up with an innovative, delicious twist on an old favorite. His Taco Casserole was the First Place winner in *American Profile*'s Get-Togethers Recipe Contest. His tasty Mexican dish incorporates cheese-flavored nacho chips, which give the entrée the flavors of a tamale. He says it's been a winner at church gatherings and at his bowling league awards dinners too.

Elvira Mileti of Columbia City, Oregon, says her husband, who is Italian, enjoys Hungarian Chicken Paprika and all the Hungarian dishes reminiscent of her own childhood. The chicken dish is always served at weddings, Mileti says, and it was a staple on her mother's dinner table at holidays as well.

It's never a problem to find family members who will enjoy Kathryn Novak's Nona's Italian Country Chicken. Novak of Northville, Michigan, says she comes from a family of six sisters and four brothers, and has eighty-one first cousins.

When she was growing up, Novak says, life centered around food and the kitchen was always filled with mouthwatering aromas. Today, Novak serves Italian Country Chicken for Christmas Eve dinner to family, including twenty-seven nieces and nephews. The delectable dish is the winner in the French's Original French Fried Onions category in *American Profile*'s Get-Togethers Recipe Contest.

No doubt Potluck Polynesian Chicken will always be a favorite of Bette Lou Wolford of Fort Morgan, Colorado. When she took it to her apartment complex community luncheon, one of the residents said he wanted to marry the person who made it. That man is now her husband of four years!

Slow Cooker Barbecue Beef Sandwiches

Eleanor Froehlich, Rochester Hills, Michigan

Serves 12

*"T*hese sandwiches are a favorite for our family picnics. I also have prepared a smaller amount for our quilting group where we serve lunch between the morning and afternoon quilting sessions. It is easy because I prepare it the day before and reheat it while we quilt in the morning."

1. Trim the excess fat from the roast and cut into large pieces. Place the roast in a 3½- to 4-quart slow cooker.

2. Combine the barbecue sauce, preserves, bell pepper, mustard, brown sugar, red onion, and salsa in a medium bowl. Pour over the beef in the slow cooker. Cover and cook on low for 9 hours or on high for 4½ to 5 hours, until the beef is very tender.

3. Remove the beef to a cutting board. Cut into thin slices or pull apart with a fork. Return the beef to the slow cooker on low for 30 minutes longer. Serve on Kaiser rolls or buns.

One 2½- to 3-pound boneless beef chuck roast
1 cup barbecue sauce
½ cup apricot preserves
½ medium green bell pepper, chopped
1 tablespoon Dijon mustard
1½ teaspoons light brown sugar
1 medium red onion, sliced paper thin
6 ounces jarred mild or medium salsa
12 Kaiser rolls or hamburger buns, split and warmed

TIPS FROM OUR TEST KITCHEN: This recipe may be doubled easily. Use an 8-quart slow cooker or two smaller ones. To easily slice the onion paper thin, use a food processor.

Slow Cooker Beef Barbecue

Jill Carrion, St. Cloud, Florida

"When I take this beef barbecue to a gathering, someone always asks for the recipe."

½ teaspoon garlic salt

One 2- to 3-pound boneless beef
   chuck roast

1 large onion, chopped

1 medium celery stalk, chopped

2 tablespoons dark brown sugar

1 cup ketchup

¼ cup lemon juice

3 tablespoons Worcestershire sauce

2 tablespoons cider vinegar

1 tablespoon liquid smoke

¼ cup all-purpose flour

6 to 8 hamburger buns, warmed

1. Sprinkle the garlic salt over the chuck roast. Place the roast in the bottom of a greased 3½- to 4-quart slow cooker. Top the beef with the onion and celery.

2. Combine the brown sugar, ketchup, lemon juice, Worcestershire sauce, vinegar, and liquid smoke in a small bowl. Pour over the top of the beef. Cover and cook on low for 8 hours, or until the beef is tender.

3. Dissolve the flour in ¼ cup water in a small bowl. Remove the beef from the slow cooker and place on a cutting board.

4. Stir the flour mixture into the sauce in the slow cooker. Shred the beef with a fork and return to the slow cooker. Cook on high for 30 minutes. Serve on hamburger buns.

Beef and Noodles

Karla Myers, Cedar Rapids, Iowa

Serves 6 to 8

"We Iowans love our casseroles, and coming from a small town, I never go anywhere empty-handed. This is the dish I make when we celebrate the good times, to comfort a family when someone passes on, or when we just feel like having a potluck. It's my most popular comfort food."

1. Quarter one of the onions; place it in a 3½- to 4-quart slow cooker. Add the steak, Greek seasoning, and ¼ cup water. Cover and cook on low for 8 hours or on high for 4 hours, until the sirloin is tender. Remove and discard the onion and remove any fat from the cooking liquid. Reserve the sirloin and cooking liquid in the slow cooker. Shred the beef using two forks. Maintain the temperature on low.

2. Prepare the noodles according to the package directions. Keep warm.

3. Melt the butter and olive oil in a large skillet over medium heat. Slice the remaining onion and add to the skillet. Cook until the onion slices are brown, 12 to 15 minutes. Add the wine and scrape the pan to loosen the browned bits. Add the garlic.

4. Combine the cornstarch with ½ cup of the beef broth in a small bowl. Add to the skillet with the remaining broth. Bring to a boil over medium-high heat and cook for 5 to 7 minutes, until thickened, stirring frequently.

2 large yellow onions
1½ pounds boneless sirloin steak
1 tablespoon Greek seasoning
1 pound uncooked extra-wide egg noodles
¼ cup (½ stick) butter
2 tablespoons olive oil
¼ cup red wine
12 garlic cloves, minced (about 2 tablespoons)
3 tablespoons cornstarch

continued

One 32-ounce carton beef broth

2 cups heavy cream

Salt and pepper

5. Add the cream to the pan and cook for 5 minutes, or until slightly thickened. Season with salt and pepper. Remove and discard the sliced onions, if desired. Pour the sauce over the beef. Serve over the egg noodles.

TIPS FROM OUR TEST KITCHEN: For a variation, add the cooked noodles to the slow cooker and stir to blend.

Hungarian Goulash

Josephine Brody, Donora, Pennsylvania

Serves 6

"I've been making this roast for fifty years and it is always a big hit."

1. Combine the ketchup, Worcestershire sauce, brown sugar, paprika, mustard, salt, and 1½ cups water in a medium bowl. Stir until well blended.

2. Heat the olive oil in a Dutch oven over medium-high heat. Working in batches, brown the beef cubes, stirring occasionally. Remove the beef with a slotted spoon and set aside on a separate plate.

3. Reduce the heat to medium. Add the onions to the pan drippings and cook until translucent, about 4 minutes, stirring frequently. Add the garlic and cook for 30 seconds, stirring constantly.

4. Add the beef, any accumulated juices, and the ketchup mixture to the Dutch oven. Increase the heat to high and bring to a boil. Reduce the heat, cover tightly, and simmer until the beef is very tender, 2 to 2½ hours, stirring occasionally.

5. Combine the cornstarch and ¼ cup water in a small bowl; stir until completely dissolved. Add to the beef mixture and stir to blend. Bring to a simmer and cook for 5 minutes, stirring frequently. Serve over egg noodles or mashed potatoes.

¾ cup ketchup

2 tablespoons Worcestershire sauce

2 tablespoons dark brown sugar

2 tablespoons paprika

1 teaspoon dry mustard

1 teaspoon salt

¼ cup olive oil

2½ pounds boneless beef chuck roast, cut into 1½-inch cubes

2 medium onions, chopped

2 garlic cloves, minced

2 teaspoons cornstarch

Cooked egg noodles or mashed potatoes

Italian Subs au Jus

Jan Gorecki, Montague, Michigan

Serves 8 to 12

"*I* used to take this to potlucks at work and never had any leftovers. I made it for a friend's son, and it became a staple in his fraternity house."

3 to 4 pounds boneless beef roast
One 16-ounce jar pepperoncini (sweet Italian peppers) with juice
Two 14-ounce cans low-sodium beef broth
1½ tablespoons dried oregano
Mini submarine buns or Italian bread

1. The day before serving, place the roast, pepperoncini, beef broth, and oregano in a 3½- to 4-quart slow cooker. Cover tightly and cook on low for 10 hours, or until the roast is very tender.

2. Remove the roast and peppers to a cutting board, reserving the cooking liquid. Shred the beef with a fork and remove the stems from the peppers. Return the beef and peppers to the slow cooker and refrigerate overnight.

3. Remove the fat from the top of the beef mixture and reheat in the slow cooker on high. Serve with mini sub buns or warmed Italian bread. Serve the juice in individual small bowls for dipping.

TIPS FROM OUR TEST KITCHEN: This recipe is just as good with venison.

Sunday Roast

Donna Roberts, Shumway, Illinois

Serves 8 to 10

"I have served this roast many times when having friends and family for dinner. Everyone raves and wants the recipe. It is quick and easy. Anyone would be proud to serve it."

1. Preheat the oven to 325°F.

2. Place the roast on a large sheet of heavy-duty foil. Coat the entire roast with the horseradish. Sprinkle the onion soup mix over the top. Tightly seal the foil and place the roast in a Dutch oven; cover tightly.

3. Bake for 1¾ to 2 hours, to the desired degree of doneness. Let stand for 10 minutes before slicing. The roast will continue to cook while resting. Slice thinly and serve with pan drippings.

One 3- to 4-pound eye-of-round or rump roast

One 5-ounce bottle prepared horseradish sauce

One 1-ounce envelope dry onion soup mix

TIPS FROM OUR TEST KITCHEN: You cannot taste the horseradish after the roast is baked.

Teriyaki Pot Roast

Donna Roberts, Shumway, Illinois

Serves 8 to 10

"I have had this recipe for many years, and it's always a hit when I serve it to friends and family."

2 tablespoons vegetable oil

3 pounds rump or eye-of-round roast

Salt and pepper

1 medium onion, chopped

1 tablespoon dark brown sugar

1 tablespoon cornstarch

1½ teaspoons beef bouillon granules

½ teaspoon ground ginger

¼ cup soy sauce

One 8-ounce can sliced water chestnuts, drained

1 pound whole carrots, cut into 3-inch pieces

4 cups hot cooked rice, optional

1. Preheat the oven to 350°F. Heat the oil in a Dutch oven over medium-high heat.

2. Season the roast with salt and pepper. Place in the Dutch oven with the onion and brown the roast on all sides, stirring the onion occasionally.

3. Combine the brown sugar, cornstarch, bouillon, ginger, soy sauce, and ¾ cup water in a small bowl. Whisk until the cornstarch is completely dissolved. Add the water chestnuts and pour the mixture over the roast. Bake, covered, for 1 hour.

4. Add the carrots and cook for 45 minutes, or until tender. Remove the roast from the oven and let stand for 10 minutes. Remove to a cutting board and slice the beef. Arrange on a serving platter with the carrots surrounding the roast. Pour the sauce in a gravy boat or pitcher and serve alongside. Serve with hot cooked rice, if using.

Fontilla's Swiss Steak and Gravy

Dan Sweeney, Green River, Wyoming

Serves 4 to 5

"*T*his recipe was originally my mom's. I've added to it a bit for those who like it hot. Coming from a family of ten, we start with a lean and less expensive cut of meat—round steaks."

1. Preheat the oven to 325°F.

2. Beat the eggs in a shallow bowl with a fork. Combine the flour, garlic powder, salt, and pepper in a separate shallow bowl.

3. Heat 3 tablespoons of the olive oil in a large ovenproof skillet over medium heat. Dip the steaks into the beaten eggs and then dredge in the flour mixture. Working in two batches, brown the steaks in the hot oil for 2 to 3 minutes on each side. Remove to a platter.

4. Heat the remaining 1 tablespoon olive oil in the skillet. Add the bell peppers and onion and cook over medium-high heat for 5 minutes, stirring frequently. Return the steaks to the skillet with the vegetables. Pour the tomatoes evenly over the steaks.

5. Bake, uncovered, for 2 hours, or until the beef is very tender. Remove half of the vegetable mixture and purée in a blender to make gravy for the mashed potatoes, if using.

2 eggs

1 cup all-purpose flour

1 tablespoon garlic powder

1 teaspoon salt

1 teaspoon black pepper

¼ cup olive oil

5 eye-of-round steaks (1¼ pounds)

1 medium red bell pepper, coarsely chopped

1 medium orange bell pepper, coarsely chopped

1 medium yellow bell pepper, coarsely chopped

1 small onion, chopped

One 14-ounce can Italian-style stewed tomatoes, undrained

One 10-ounce can mild tomatoes with green chiles, undrained

Mashed potatoes, optional

TIPS FROM OUR TEST KITCHEN: For a thinner consistency, add ¼ to ⅓ cup water to the skillet before baking and season with additional salt and pepper.

Baked Spaghetti

Tammy Upchurch, Monticello, Kentucky

Serves 10 to 12

"I have served this Baked Spaghetti for Sunday family dinners, office parties, and holiday get-togethers. It is always a big hit, and it's so easy to make."

One 12-ounce package uncooked spaghetti, broken in half

3 pounds ground beef

1 large onion, finely chopped

Two 26-ounce cans spaghetti sauce

One 7-ounce can sliced mushrooms, drained

One 2-ounce can sliced black olives, drained, optional

1 medium green bell pepper, chopped

One 14-ounce can diced tomatoes, drained

2 teaspoons dried oregano, or to taste

¼ teaspoon dried red pepper flakes, or to taste

1 teaspoon salt

1 teaspoon black pepper

One 3-ounce package small pepperoni slices (50-count package)

4 cups shredded mozzarella

1. Preheat the oven to 350°F. Grease a 13×9-inch metal cake pan.

2. Cook the spaghetti in a stockpot according to the package directions. Drain well and return the pasta to the pot off the heat.

3. Heat a Dutch oven over high heat. Spray with nonstick cooking spray, add the ground beef and onion, and cook until browned, stirring constantly. Drain and add to the pasta in the stockpot. Stir in the spaghetti sauce, mushrooms, olives, if using, bell pepper, tomatoes, oregano, red pepper flakes, salt, and black pepper; toss to blend.

4. Spoon the mixture into the prepared pan. Top with the pepperoni and sprinkle evenly with the mozzarella. Bake, uncovered, for 25 minutes, or until the cheese is melted.

TIPS FROM OUR TEST KITCHEN: Use a metal cake pan rather than a glass baking dish, since it is larger. If a cake pan is not available, reduce the amount of pasta to 8 to 10 ounces.

Beef and Cheese Casserole

Carole Bruere, Albuquerque, New Mexico

Serves 8

"*T*his casserole has always been great comfort food on chilly nights. In 1966, this recipe won first place and $6 at the Wheatland, Wyoming, County Fair. It has been winning over family and friends ever since."

1. Preheat the oven to 350°F. Grease a 3-quart glass baking dish or a 13×9-inch baking dish.

2. Cook the noodles according to the package directions; drain well and set aside.

3. Heat a large skillet over medium-high heat. Add the ground beef and onion and cook until browned, stirring frequently. Remove the skillet from the heat; drain any excess liquid. Add the tomato sauce, tomato paste, salt, and pepper; mix well.

4. Combine the cream cheese, cottage cheese, sour cream, bell pepper, and green onions in a large bowl; mix well.

5. Layer half of the noodles in the prepared pan. Spoon the cheese mixture over the noodles. Using the back of a spoon, spread the mixture evenly. Top with the remaining noodles. Spoon the ground beef mixture on top of the noodles. Bake for 35 to 40 minutes, until thoroughly heated.

12 ounces uncooked egg noodles

1½ pounds ground beef

1 medium onion, chopped

Two 8-ounce cans tomato sauce (plain or with basil, garlic, and oregano)

One 6-ounce can tomato paste

1 teaspoon salt

1 teaspoon black pepper

Two 8-ounce packages cream cheese, softened

1 cup cottage cheese

¼ cup sour cream

½ medium green bell pepper, finely chopped

4 green onions, minced (white and green parts)

Fried Onion Burger

Willis J. Welch, Shelbyville, Tennessee

Serves 6

"I've shared this recipe at all family cookouts."

2 pounds ground beef

Two 2-ounce cans French's Original
　　French Fried Onions

1½ teaspoons salt

¾ teaspoon black pepper

6 hamburger buns, warmed, optional

Preheat the grill or a broiler on high. Combine the ground beef, French fried onions, salt, and pepper in a large bowl. Shape into 6 patties. Cook on the grill or broil for 5 to 6 minutes on each side, to the desired degree of doneness. Serve on hamburger buns, if using, with condiments of your choice.

Little Cheddar Meat Loaves

Chicky Washam, Odessa, Missouri

"I take these Little Cheddar Meat Loaves to a lot of church dinners, and there are never any leftovers."

1. Preheat the oven to 350°F. Grease a 13×9-inch baking dish.

2. Beat the egg and milk in a large bowl. Add the Cheddar, oats, onion, and salt; mix well. Add the ground beef and mix well. Shape into 8 equal loaves. Place in the prepared dish.

3. Combine the ketchup, brown sugar, and mustard in a small bowl; mix well. Spoon over the loaves. Bake, uncovered, for 45 minutes, or until no longer pink in the center.

1 egg

¾ cup milk

1 cup shredded Cheddar

½ cup quick-cooking oats

1 medium onion, finely chopped

1 teaspoon salt

1 pound lean ground beef

⅔ cup ketchup

½ cup packed dark brown sugar

1½ teaspoons prepared mustard

Sloppy Joes

Colleen Ostergaard, Kaysville, Utah

Serves 20

"This recipe is a favorite for get-togethers at our cabin. Our family enjoys putting the Sloppy Joes on buns or over chips. It goes with every type of picnic food."

4 pounds ground beef

¼ cup dried onions

One 24-ounce bottle ketchup

2 tablespoons all-purpose flour

2 tablespoons cider vinegar

2 tablespoons lemon juice

¼ cup Worcestershire sauce

¾ cup packed dark brown sugar

1 teaspoon dry mustard

20 hamburger buns, warmed

1. Heat a stockpot over medium-high heat. Spray with nonstick cooking spray. Add the ground beef and onions and cook until the beef is browned. Drain and return the beef mixture to the stockpot.

2. Add the ketchup, flour, vinegar, lemon juice, Worcestershire sauce, brown sugar, dry mustard, and 1 cup water. Bring to a boil, reduce the heat, and simmer, uncovered, for 20 minutes, stirring occasionally. Serve with hamburger buns.

TIPS FROM OUR TEST KITCHEN: The Sloppy Joes can be made ahead of time, frozen in zip-top plastic bags, and reheated when ready to serve.

Stuffed Peppers

Judith Bonsall, Hillsdale, Michigan

"This recipe came from my aunt many years ago. To store for later use, place the cooked peppers on baking sheets and freeze. When frozen, transfer to zip-top freezer bags. They won't stick together so you can remove just the amount that you need."

1. Preheat the oven to 350°F. Grease a 13×9-inch baking dish.

2. Heat a large skillet over medium-high heat. Add the ground beef, sausage, and onion and cook until the ground beef is no longer pink and the sausage is barely pink, stirring frequently. Remove from the heat, drain, and return the meat to the skillet. Add the rice, sugar, salt, and pepper.

3. Spoon equal amounts (about 1 cup) of the mixture into each bell pepper. Arrange in the prepared dish.

4. Combine the soup, vinegar, and 2 cups of water in a medium bowl; whisk until smooth. Pour over the peppers and dot with the butter.

5. Bake, covered, for 45 minutes. Uncover and bake for 15 minutes longer, or until the peppers are tender. Let stand for 10 to 15 minutes before placing on a serving platter.

1 pound ground beef

8 ounces mild or hot Italian sausage, casings removed, or bulk pork sausage

1 medium onion, finely chopped

2 cups cooked rice

1 tablespoon sugar

1 teaspoon salt

¼ teaspoon black pepper

6 large green bell peppers, tops and seeds removed

One 10-ounce can tomato soup

2 tablespoons cider vinegar

2 tablespoons butter

Taco Casserole

Edgar D. Galbraith, Jacksonville, North Carolina

"*I*'ve very successfully served this Taco Casserole at church gatherings and at my bowling league awards dinners."

1 pound lean ground beef

2 tablespoons olive oil

1 medium onion, finely chopped

1 garlic clove, minced

4 ounces portobello mushrooms, coarsely chopped

One 1-ounce package taco seasoning mix

¼ teaspoon salt

⅛ teaspoon black pepper

One 14-ounce can diced tomatoes or one 10-ounce can diced tomatoes with green chiles, undrained

One 8-ounce can tomato sauce

One 4-ounce bag cheese-flavored nacho chips

2 tablespoons chopped cilantro

2 cups shredded Cheddar

One 2-ounce can French's Original French Fried Onions

Cilantro sprigs

1. Preheat the oven to 350°F. Grease a 13×9-inch baking dish.

2. Brown the ground beef in the olive oil in a large skillet over medium-high heat. Reduce the heat to medium and add the onion, garlic, and mushrooms; cook until the onions are translucent, about 5 minutes, stirring frequently.

3. Add the taco seasoning mix, salt, and pepper; mix well. Stir in the tomatoes and tomato sauce; simmer, uncovered, for 10 minutes. Remove from the heat and stir in the whole nacho chips and chopped cilantro. Mix gently but thoroughly until the chips are coated with the sauce.

4. Spoon the mixture into the prepared baking dish. Sprinkle with the Cheddar and French fried onions. Bake for 18 to 20 minutes, until the onions are lightly browned. Garnish with cilantro sprigs.

TIPS FROM OUR TEST KITCHEN: This dish is very popular with all ages. The nacho chips break down and create a tamale-flavored entrée.
FIRST PLACE WINNER IN AMERICAN PROFILE *MAGAZINE'S GET-TOGETHERS RECIPE CONTEST*

Grand Taco Salad

Helen Chitwood, McKinleyville, California

Serves 12 to 16

"*O*ur family loves this easy, cool salad when we get together. Since it is prepared at the last minute, there is more time for us to visit."

1. Heat a large skillet over medium-high heat until hot. Add the ground beef and taco seasoning mix and cook until the beef is browned, stirring frequently. Set aside to cool completely.

2. Combine the iceberg lettuce, romaine lettuce, onion, tomatoes, cucumber, beans, avocado, corn, celery, jalapeño, if using, and dressing in a 9-quart salad bowl or two 5-quart salad bowls. Sprinkle evenly with the beef mixture, chips, and cheese. Toss, if desired, before serving. Serve immediately for peak flavors and texture.

1 pound ground beef
One 1-ounce package taco
    seasoning mix
One 10-ounce bag iceberg lettuce
One 10-ounce bag romaine lettuce
1 medium red onion, chopped
2 medium tomatoes, chopped
½ medium cucumber, peeled, if desired,
    and finely chopped
One 15-ounce can dark red kidney
    beans, rinsed and drained
1 medium avocado, peeled, pitted, and
    chopped
1 cup frozen corn kernels, thawed
2 medium celery stalks, thinly sliced
1 medium jalapeño chile, seeded and
    finely chopped, optional
One 16-ounce bottle Italian dressing
2 cups crushed corn chips
1 to 2 cups shredded Mexican cheese
    blend or Cheddar

TIPS FROM OUR TEST KITCHEN: All of the ingredients can be cooked or chopped ahead of time and combined in a large bowl just before serving. Pass bowls of mild or spicy salsa for topping, if desired.

Zippy Porcupines

Virginia Breedlove, Wharton, Texas

Serves 4 to 5

"We love this dish. The crushed onions make it. This is a 'must-bring' at our family reunions. They won't let us in without it."

1 pound ground beef

½ cup uncooked long grain rice

1 medium green bell pepper, diced

1 medium red bell pepper, diced

1 medium onion, diced

1 teaspoon garlic powder

1 teaspoon salt

¾ teaspoon black pepper

One 6-ounce can French's Original
   French Fried Onions, finely crushed

2 cups tomato juice

2 teaspoons Tabasco sauce

1. Preheat the oven to 350°F. Grease a 13×9-inch baking dish.

2. Combine the ground beef, rice, bell peppers, onion, garlic powder, salt, and pepper in a large mixing bowl. Add half of the French fried onions; mix well.

3. Shape the mixture into 20 golf-ball-size balls. Roll in the remaining French fried onions. Arrange in the prepared dish. Combine the tomato juice and Tabasco in a small bowl; mix well. Pour over the meatballs.

4. Bake, uncovered, for 1 hour and 15 minutes, or until the rice is tender.

Baked Swiss Chicken

Verma Logan, Ardmore, Oklahoma

Serves 8

"*I* just moved from California to Oklahoma. When I lived in California, I was active in several organizations, and whenever we had a potluck I would make Baked Swiss Chicken, which always went over big."

1. Preheat the oven to 350°F. Grease a 13×9-inch baking dish.

2. Arrange the chicken in the prepared dish. Top each piece with a slice of cheese.

3. Combine the soup and wine in a small bowl and whisk until well blended. Spoon the sauce over the chicken. Sprinkle the stuffing mix on top and drizzle with the melted butter.

4. Bake for 50 minutes, or until the chicken is golden and no longer pink in the center.

8 boneless, skinless chicken breasts, rinsed and patted dry (6 ounces each)

8 slices Swiss cheese

One 10-ounce can cream of chicken soup

¼ cup dry white wine

1 cup herb-seasoned stuffing mix, crushed

¼ cup (½ stick) butter, melted

TIPS FROM OUR TEST KITCHEN: The chicken can be prepared ahead of time, refrigerated, and baked just before serving. Leftovers freeze well after baking. Double or triple the sauce and pass with the chicken.

Chicken with Cilantro

Carlene Carter, Lincoln, Illinois

Serves 8

"We are very fond of cilantro, so we developed this dish. The recipe is a favorite of ours that is simple to make, serves easily, is very tasty, and is a little bit different."

CHICKEN

3 bone-in chicken breasts

Two 28-ounce cans whole tomatoes, undrained

4 garlic cloves, minced

2 teaspoons salt, or to taste

2 medium green bell peppers, sliced

1 large onion, sliced

2 teaspoons paprika

½ cup chopped cilantro, or to taste

YELLOW RICE

2 teaspoons salt

2 tablespoons extra virgin olive oil

½ teaspoon ground turmeric

2 cups uncooked basmati rice

1. To prepare the chicken, place the chicken in a stockpot. Place the tomatoes in a bowl and crush slightly. Pour over the chicken. Add the garlic and salt. Bring to a boil, reduce the heat, and simmer with the lid slightly ajar, until the chicken easily pulls away from the bones, about 50 minutes, stirring occasionally. Add a small amount of water if the mixture gets too thick. Remove the chicken and set aside on a plate to cool.

2. Add the bell peppers, onion, and paprika to the stockpot. Return to a simmer and cook, uncovered, until the onion is tender and the sauce is slightly thickened. Bone the cooled chicken and tear it into bite-size pieces. Return the chicken to the stockpot and add the cilantro and season with salt.

3. To prepare the rice, combine 3½ cups water, the salt, olive oil, and turmeric in a large saucepan. Bring to a boil. Stir in the rice, return to a boil, and reduce the heat. Cover tightly and simmer for 15 minutes, or until the liquid is absorbed. Fluff with a fork before serving.

Creamy Chicken with Noodles

Linda Wydra, Wapwallopen, Pennsylvania

Serves 6

"*T*his recipe looks great served on a big platter. It is very pretty and very good."

1. Cook the noodles according to the package directions. Pound the chicken to ¼-inch thickness. Sprinkle with the salt and pepper.

2. Heat 2 tablespoons of the olive oil in a large skillet over medium heat. Working in batches, cook the chicken until it is golden and no longer pink in the center, about 3 minutes on each side. Remove from the skillet to a plate, cover, and keep warm. Repeat with the remaining chicken breasts.

3. Heat the remaining 2 tablespoons olive oil in the skillet. Add the mushrooms and garlic. Cook until the mushrooms are tender, about 3 minutes, stirring frequently.

4. Add the soups, half-and-half, chicken broth, and chili powder; mix well. Cook until thoroughly heated, about 2 minutes. Stir in ¼ cup of the parsley.

5. Drain the noodles and arrange on a large serving platter. Arrange the chicken on top of the pasta. Pour the sauce evenly over the chicken and sprinkle with the remaining parsley.

8 ounces uncooked egg noodles

6 boneless, skinless chicken breasts, rinsed and patted dry

½ teaspoon salt

¼ teaspoon black pepper

¼ cup olive oil

6 ounces fresh mushrooms, sliced

2 garlic cloves, minced

One 10-ounce can cream of chicken soup

One 10-ounce can cream of mushroom soup

¾ cup half-and-half

¼ cup chicken broth or Marsala wine

¼ teaspoon chili powder

½ cup finely chopped parsley

Everyone's Favorite Chicken

Elaine Arnold, Altus, Oklahoma

Serves 4 to 5

"*L*uncheon potlucks are a favorite activity at my workplace. When I brought this casserole in during the holidays, everyone loved it. Any leftovers went home with whoever got there first!"

3 cups diced cooked chicken

2 medium celery stalks, finely chopped

One 8-ounce can sliced water chestnuts, drained

½ cup sliced almonds

One 2-ounce jar pimientos, undrained

1 tablespoon minced onion

1 cup mayonnaise

2 tablespoons lemon juice

1 teaspoon salt

1 teaspoon black pepper

1 cup French's Original French Fried Onions

8 ounces Cheddar, shredded

1. Preheat the oven to 350°F. Grease an 11×7-inch baking dish.

2. Combine the chicken, celery, water chestnuts, almonds, pimientos, onion, mayonnaise, lemon juice, salt, and pepper in a large bowl; mix well.

3. Place in the prepared dish and top with the French fried onions and Cheddar. Bake, covered, for 30 minutes, or until the cheese is melted.

TIPS FROM OUR TEST KITCHEN: If using precooked chicken, omit ½ teaspoon of the salt.

Fried Onion Crusted Chicken

Mrs. Clay Rowland, Marion, Virginia

Serves 4

*"T*his chicken recipe is special. You will enjoy it."

1. Preheat the oven to 350°F. Grease a 13×9-inch baking dish.

2. Pound the chicken with a meat mallet to ¼-inch thickness. Season with salt and pepper.

3. Combine the butter, mustard, and Worcestershire sauce in a shallow bowl. Place the crushed French fried onions in a separate shallow dish. Dip the chicken in the butter mixture and then coat with the crushed onions.

4. Arrange the chicken in the prepared dish. Pour any of the remaining butter mixture over the chicken and top with crushed onions.

5. Bake for 25 minutes, or until the chicken is golden brown and no longer pink in the center.

4 boneless, skinless chicken breasts, rinsed and patted dry
Salt
Black pepper
½ cup (1 stick) butter, melted
1 teaspoon dry mustard
1 teaspoon Worcestershire sauce
Two 2-ounce cans French's Original French Fried Onions, finely crushed

TIPS FROM OUR TEST KITCHEN: This chicken is sophisticated, yet kid friendly.

Hungarian Chicken Paprika

Elvira Mileti, Columbia City, Oregon

Serves 4 to 6

"*T*his is a famous Hungarian meal. It is always served at weddings, and my mother served it on all holidays. She and my father came to America from Hungary in the early 1900s. My Italian husband of almost fifty years enjoys all Hungarian dishes."

¼ cup vegetable shortening

1 medium onion, chopped

1 tablespoon paprika

1 teaspoon black pepper

2 teaspoons salt

One 4- to 5-pound chicken, cut up

1 cup sour cream

Egg noodles or dumplings, cooked

1. Melt the shortening in a large skillet over medium-high heat. Add the onion and cook until the onion begins to brown, about 6 minutes. Add the paprika, pepper, and salt; stir to blend.

2. Add the chicken to the skillet and brown for 10 minutes, turning frequently. Add 1½ cups water, bring to a boil, reduce the heat, cover tightly, and simmer until tender, about 45 minutes.

3. Remove the chicken to a shallow serving bowl. Add the sour cream to the pan drippings and whisk until well blended. Pour over the chicken. Serve with egg noodles or dumplings.

Mushroom and Italian Herb Chicken

Dawn Onuffer, Crestview, Florida

Serves 10 to 12

"There is very little prep work involved in this recipe, so it is ideal to prepare in the morning and serve later that night. Cooking all day really infuses the flavors together."

1. Place the chicken in a 6-quart slow cooker. Top with the mushrooms, bell peppers, and onion.

2. Combine the stewed tomatoes, tomato paste, cornstarch, sugar, oregano, red pepper flakes, salt, and black pepper in a bowl; mix well. Pour over the chicken and vegetables.

3. Cover and cook on low for 9 to 10 hours or on high for 5 hours, until the chicken is thoroughly cooked and the onion is tender.

4. Cook the pasta according to the package directions. Drain and transfer to a serving platter. Spoon the chicken and sauce over the pasta.

10 boneless, skinless chicken thighs, or 5 boneless, skinless chicken breasts
1 pound fresh mushrooms. sliced
¼ medium red bell pepper, finely chopped
¼ medium green bell pepper, finely chopped
¼ medium onion, finely chopped
Two 14-ounce cans stewed tomatoes, undrained
One 6-ounce can tomato paste
2 tablespoons cornstarch
1 tablespoon sugar
1 teaspoon dried oregano
¼ to ½ teaspoon dried red pepper flakes
½ teaspoon salt
½ teaspoon black pepper
1¼ pounds uncooked penne or any variety pasta

Nona's Italian Country Chicken

Kathryn Novak, Northville, Michigan

Serves 6

"*I* come from a family of six sisters, four brothers, and eighty-one first cousins. Life centered around food. Our kitchen was always filled with mouthwatering aromas. Nona's Italian Country Chicken is a favorite I serve for Christmas Eve dinner. It is very simple and quite delicious. The kids (I have twenty-seven nieces and nephews) and adults all love it."

3 eggs

6 boneless, skinless chicken breasts, quartered

2½ cups dry Italian bread crumbs

½ cup (1 stick) butter plus 1 to 2 tablespoons, if needed

2 tablespoons extra virgin olive oil

1½ teaspoons dried Italian seasoning

2 large green bell peppers, thinly sliced

One 7-ounce can sliced mushrooms, well drained

2 cups chicken broth

1. Beat the eggs in a large, shallow dish. Arrange the chicken in the dish, turn to coat with the eggs, cover, and refrigerate overnight.

2. Preheat the oven to 350°F. Grease a 13×9-inch baking dish.

3. Place the bread crumbs in a shallow pan. Coat the chicken with the bread crumbs.

4. Melt ½ cup butter in a large skillet over medium heat. Working in batches, cook the chicken until browned, about 2 minutes per side. Add 1 to 2 tablespoons butter, if needed. Remove the chicken to the prepared pan.

5. Add the olive oil and Italian seasoning to the skillet drippings and heat over medium heat. Add the bell pepper strips and cook until brown, about 12 minutes, stirring frequently.

6. Sprinkle the peppers and mushrooms evenly over the chicken. Add ½ cup of the chicken broth to the skillet, scraping to loosen browned bits; pour the broth from the skillet and the remaining broth over the chicken. Top with the shredded cheese.

7. Bake, uncovered, for 30 minutes. Sprinkle the French fried onions evenly over the top and bake for 15 minutes longer, or until golden.

2 cups shredded Monterey Jack

One 2-ounce can French's Original French Fried Onions

TIPS FROM OUR TEST KITCHEN: This dish may be doubled easily by using two 13×9-inch pans and browning in two large skillets. French's Original French Fried Onions category winner in *American Profile* magazine's Get-Togethers Recipe Contest

Potluck Polynesian Chicken

Bette Lou Wolford, Fort Morgan, Colorado

Serves 6 to 8

"I have made this dish many times for various potlucks. One time when I made it for our apartment community luncheon, a man declared that he wanted to marry the person who made it. That man is now my husband of more than four years!"

1 cup buttermilk

1 cup all-purpose flour

1 teaspoon salt

¼ teaspoon black pepper

One 3- to 4-pound chicken, cut up

1 cup peanut oil

One 20-ounce can pineapple chunks in juice

1 cup sugar

2 tablespoons cornstarch

¾ cup cider vinegar

1 tablespoon soy sauce

1 teaspoon chicken bouillon granules

¼ teaspoon ground ginger

1 medium green bell pepper, sliced into thin strips

Sliced pimientos, optional

Cooked rice, optional

TIPS FROM OUR TEST KITCHEN: Boneless, skinless chicken thighs and/or breasts may be used in place of the whole chicken, if desired.

1. Preheat the oven to 350°F. Grease a 13×9-inch baking pan.

2. Pour the buttermilk into a shallow bowl. Combine the flour, salt, and pepper in a separate shallow bowl. Dip the chicken in the buttermilk and dredge in the flour mixture. Place the chicken on a baking sheet or piece of foil.

3. Heat the peanut oil in a large skillet over medium-high heat. Brown the chicken in the oil and remove to the prepared pan.

4. Drain the pineapple and reserve the juice in a 2-cup measuring cup. Add enough water to equal 1½ cups liquid.

5. Combine the sugar and cornstarch in a medium saucepan. Stir in the pineapple liquid, vinegar, soy sauce, bouillon granules, and ginger. Stir until the cornstarch is completely dissolved. Bring to a boil and cook for 2 minutes, stirring constantly.

6. Pour the sauce over the chicken and bake, uncovered, for 30 minutes. Add the pineapple, bell pepper strips, and pimientos, if using. Bake for 15 minutes longer, or until the chicken is tender and no longer pink in the center. Serve over rice, if using.

Spicy Grilled Chicken

Jane Woods, Fort Worth, Texas

Serves 6

*"**B**ecause it's so common for families and friends to enjoy grilling, I developed a recipe for these events, which can either be served hot, or grilled ahead of time and served cold. I've found that chicken is always a favorite for children and adults."*

1. Combine the honey, taco seasoning mix, vinegar, orange zest, orange juice, green onions, garlic, and rosemary leaves in a shallow dish; mix well. Add the chicken and turn several times to coat with the marinade. Cover with plastic wrap and refrigerate at least 8 hours or overnight.

2. Remove the chicken; discard the marinade.

3. Preheat a grill to medium-high. Grill the chicken, covered with the grill lid, until no longer pink in the center, about 6 minutes on each side. Garnish with fresh rosemary sprigs, if using.

⅔ **cup honey**

One 1-ounce package taco or chili seasoning mix

2 tablespoons white wine vinegar

Zest of 1 medium orange

2 tablespoons orange juice

3 medium green onions, minced (white and green parts)

2 garlic cloves, minced

2 tablespoons fresh rosemary leaves, minced

6 boneless, skinless chicken breasts, rinsed and patted dry

Fresh rosemary sprigs, optional

TIPS FROM OUR TEST KITCHEN: The chicken may be broiled instead of grilled. Broil about 6 inches from the heat source for 6 minutes on each side, or until no longer pink in the center.

Turkey Tetrazzini

Bonnie Mattox, Albuquerque, New Mexico

Serves 6 to 8

"*T*urkey is popular at our house year-round. I've shared this recipe often with bridge friends and even the chef at the local senior center."

8 ounces uncooked thin spaghetti

2 cups chopped cooked turkey or
    chicken

3 tablespoons butter

8 ounces fresh mushrooms, sliced

1 medium onion, chopped

2 cups half-and-half

8 ounces Cheddar or mozzarella cheese,
    shredded (2 cups)

One 2-ounce jar diced pimientos,
    undrained

One 4-ounce can chopped green chiles,
    undrained, optional

1 cup herb stuffing mix, crushed,
    optional

1. Preheat the oven 350°F. Grease a 13×9-inch baking dish.

2. Cook the spaghetti according to the package directions in a stockpot. Remove the pot from the heat, drain, and return the pasta to the stockpot. Add the turkey; mix well. Spoon the mixture into the prepared dish.

3. Melt the butter in a large skillet over medium heat. Add the mushrooms and onion and cook until the onion is golden, about 8 minutes, stirring frequently. Stir in the half-and-half and Cheddar. Heat until the cheese melts; add the pimientos and chiles, if using.

4. Pour the cheese mixture over the pasta and turkey. Top with the stuffing mix, if using. Bake for 30 minutes.

Eggplant Parmesan with Pepperoni

Loretta Petrosky, Lower Burrell, Pennsylvania

Serves 8

"This is a great dish to take to picnics. I usually bake two and freeze one for later use."

1. Peel the eggplant and cut into ¼-inch slices. Arrange the slices on paper towels and sprinkle with the salt. Let stand for 10 to 15 minutes. Blot dry with paper towels.

2. Preheat the oven to 375°F. Grease a 13×9-inch baking dish.

3. Place the flour in a shallow bowl. Place the eggs in a second shallow bowl; beat well. Place the bread crumbs in a third shallow bowl.

4. Heat ¼ cup of the olive oil in a large skillet over medium heat. Dip each eggplant slice in the flour, eggs, and bread crumbs. Working in batches, brown the slices for 2 minutes on each side. Add the remaining ¼ cup olive oil, if needed. Make sure the oil is hot before proceeding.

5. Place a layer of browned eggplant in the prepared dish. Top with one-third of the mozzarella, chopped eggs, pepperoni, Parmesan, and spaghetti sauce. Repeat the layers twice.

6. Spray a sheet of aluminum foil with nonstick cooking spray. Cover the casserole with the sprayed side down. Bake for 35 minutes. Uncover and bake for 10 to 15 minutes longer, until thoroughly heated. Let stand for 10 minutes before serving. Sprinkle with additional Parmesan, if using.

1 medium eggplant (about 1½ pounds)

½ teaspoon salt

1 cup all-purpose flour

2 eggs

2 cups dry Italian bread crumbs

½ cup olive oil

8 ounces mozzarella cheese, shredded (2 cups)

3 hard-cooked eggs, finely chopped

2 ounces sandwich-style pepperoni slices, cut into eighths and separated

½ cup grated Parmesan or Romano, or to taste

One 24-ounce jar spaghetti sauce

Grated Parmesan, optional

Pineapple Upside-Down Ham and Onion Loaf

Patricia Lawshe, Kalispell, Montana

Serves 8

"With six children and a variety of company at all times, this loaf was a great way to stretch a meal and use leftover ham. It was always the choice to take to a 4-H get-together because it looked fancy and was easy for even the kids to make."

3 tablespoons melted butter

1/3 cup packed dark brown sugar

One 20-ounce can pineapple slices, drained (use 9 slices, save remainder for later use)

9 maraschino cherries, drained

1 pound ground cooked ham

2/3 pound freshly ground pork or bulk pork sausage

2 cups dry Italian bread crumbs

2 eggs, well beaten

1 cup milk

1 teaspoon salt

1/4 teaspoon black pepper

1/2 teaspoon dry mustard

One 2-ounce can French's Original French Fried Onions

1. Preheat the oven to 350°F.

2. Combine the butter and the brown sugar in a small bowl; mix well. Spread the mixture in the bottom of an 8-inch-square glass baking dish. Place a layer of the pineapple slices on top of the sugar mixture and place a cherry in the middle of each.

3. Combine the ham, pork, bread crumbs, eggs, milk, salt, pepper, and mustard in a medium bowl; mix well. Spread evenly on top of the fruit. Carefully press the French fried onions on top of the ham mixture to resemble a crust.

4. Cover with foil and bake on a foil-lined oven rack for 1 hour. Uncover and bake for 30 minutes longer. Run a knife carefully between the edge of the loaf and the sides of the dish. Place a platter on top of the dish and invert. Let stand for 10 minutes before cutting into squares to serve.

Turkey Tetrazzini

Bonnie Mattox, Albuquerque, New Mexico

Serves 6 to 8

"Turkey is popular at our house year-round. I've shared this recipe often with bridge friends and even the chef at the local senior center."

8 ounces uncooked thin spaghetti

2 cups chopped cooked turkey or
   chicken

3 tablespoons butter

8 ounces fresh mushrooms, sliced

1 medium onion, chopped

2 cups half-and-half

8 ounces Cheddar or mozzarella cheese,
   shredded (2 cups)

One 2-ounce jar diced pimientos,
   undrained

One 4-ounce can chopped green chiles,
   undrained, optional

1 cup herb stuffing mix, crushed,
   optional

1. Preheat the oven 350°F. Grease a 13×9-inch baking dish.

2. Cook the spaghetti according to the package directions in a stockpot. Remove the pot from the heat, drain, and return the pasta to the stockpot. Add the turkey; mix well. Spoon the mixture into the prepared dish.

3. Melt the butter in a large skillet over medium heat. Add the mushrooms and onion and cook until the onion is golden, about 8 minutes, stirring frequently. Stir in the half-and-half and Cheddar. Heat until the cheese melts; add the pimientos and chiles, if using.

4. Pour the cheese mixture over the pasta and turkey. Top with the stuffing mix, if using. Bake for 30 minutes.

Spicy Grilled Chicken

Jane Woods, Fort Worth, Texas

"*B*ecause it's so common for families and friends to enjoy grilling, I developed a recipe for these events, which can either be served hot, or grilled ahead of time and served cold. I've found that chicken is always a favorite for children and adults."

1. Combine the honey, taco seasoning mix, vinegar, orange zest, orange juice, green onions, garlic, and rosemary leaves in a shallow dish; mix well. Add the chicken and turn several times to coat with the marinade. Cover with plastic wrap and refrigerate at least 8 hours or overnight.

2. Remove the chicken; discard the marinade.

3. Preheat a grill to medium-high. Grill the chicken, covered with the grill lid, until no longer pink in the center, about 6 minutes on each side. Garnish with fresh rosemary sprigs, if using.

⅔ cup honey

One 1-ounce package taco or chili seasoning mix

2 tablespoons white wine vinegar

Zest of 1 medium orange

2 tablespoons orange juice

3 medium green onions, minced (white and green parts)

2 garlic cloves, minced

2 tablespoons fresh rosemary leaves, minced

6 boneless, skinless chicken breasts, rinsed and patted dry

Fresh rosemary sprigs, optional

TIPS FROM OUR TEST KITCHEN: The chicken may be broiled instead of grilled. Broil about 6 inches from the heat source for 6 minutes on each side, or until no longer pink in the center.

Cherry Glazed Pork Roast

Dorothy Clonch, Hopkinsville, Kentucky

Serves 12 to 14

"I have served this many times, especially at Easter and when I have company. Everyone loves it."

1. Preheat the oven to 325°F.

2. Place the roast on a rack in a shallow roasting pan. Cook, uncovered, for 2 to 2½ hours, until a meat thermometer registers 155°F.

3. Combine the cherry pie filling, raisins, lemon juice, and cinnamon in a medium bowl; mix well. Spoon the cherry glaze over the pork several times during the last 20 minutes of cooking time, reserving some for serving.

4. Remove the roast to a cutting board and let stand for 10 minutes before slicing. Heat the remaining glaze and serve with the carved roast.

One 5- to 6-pound boneless double pork loin roast, rolled and tied

One 21-ounce can cherry pie filling

¼ to ½ cup golden raisins

2 tablespoons lemon juice

½ teaspoon ground cinnamon

TIPS FROM OUR TEST KITCHEN: The roast's internal temperature will continue to rise 5 to 10 degrees after it is removed from the oven.

Pork Chops Delight

Mrs. Norvell Lasseter, Waco, Texas

Serves 4 to 6

"*O*ur family is of German heritage and this is a favorite at our reunions."

½ cup all-purpose flour
6 lean breakfast pork chops (about 1¾
    pounds total), about ½ inch thick
Salt and pepper
½ cup canola oil
Two 14-ounce cans sauerkraut,
    undrained

1. Place the flour in a shallow bowl. Season the pork chops with salt and pepper, and dredge in the flour, shaking off any excess.

2. Heat the oil in a large skillet over medium-high heat. Working in two batches, brown the pork chops in the skillet about 3 minutes per side. Remove to a plate. Pour off excess grease from the skillet, leaving the pan residue.

3. Spoon 1 can sauerkraut into the skillet and place the pork chops on top. Spoon the remaining can of sauerkraut over the pork chops. Pour 1¾ cups water evenly over the top.

4. Bring to a boil over medium-high heat. Reduce the heat, cover tightly, and simmer until the liquid evaporates and the pork is very tender, about 50 minutes.

Nona's Italian Country Chicken (page 140)

Old-Fashioned Oatmeal Cake
with Broiled Topping (page 183)

Olive Salsa (page 30)

Old-Fashioned Orange Layer Cake (page 184)

Pear Rum Cake with Chocolate Topping (page 186)

Bell Peppers with Peanuts and Water Chestnuts (page 86)

Potluck Polynesian Chicken (page 142)

Superb Red Pepper Soup (page 63)

Roasted Eggplant Soup with Garlic Cream (page 60)

Scarborough Fair Herb Bread (page 49)

Sun-Dried Tomato Pesto Pasta (page 109)

Shrimp Feast (page 157)

Spanish Rice (page 104)   *Spicy Grilled Chicken (page 143)*

Fresh Strawberry French Toast (page 16)

Strawberry Orange Salad with Glazed Almonds (page 75)

Taco Casserole (page 130)

Tomato Pie (page 163)

Pork Loin in Creamy Sauce

Jan Christofferson, Eagle River, Wisconsin

Serves 6

"I make this often for relatives and friends. It is a great get-together main dish. I serve it over brown rice, white rice, or whole wheat noodles."

1. Preheat the oven to 325°F. Grease a 13×9-inch baking dish.

2. Place the pork slices on a cutting board, cover with plastic wrap or wax paper, and pound to ¾-inch thickness with a meat mallet.

3. Combine the eggs, 1½ tablespoons cold water, the garlic powder, rosemary, salt, and pepper in a shallow bowl; mix well. Place the bread crumbs in a second shallow bowl. Dip the pork slices into the egg mixture and then the bread crumbs.

4. Melt 2 tablespoons of the butter in a large skillet over medium heat. Add 3 of the pork slices and cook for 5 minutes on each side, or until golden brown. Transfer to the prepared dish. Repeat.

5. Melt the remaining 2 tablespoons butter in the skillet. Add the mushrooms and cook until the mushrooms are soft, 3 to 4 minutes, stirring frequently. Whisk the soup, sour cream, and sherry in a medium bowl and add to the mushrooms; mix well.

6. Pour the mixture evenly over the pork slices. Cover and bake for 1 hour and 15 minutes, or until the pork is very tender and the sauce is slightly thickened and bubbly.

2 pounds boneless pork loin, cut into 6 slices

2 eggs, slightly beaten

⅛ teaspoon garlic powder

½ teaspoon dried rosemary, finely chopped

¼ teaspoon salt

½ teaspoon black pepper

1 cup dry Italian bread crumbs

6 tablespoons butter

8 ounces fresh mushrooms, sliced

One 10-ounce can cream of chicken soup

1 cup sour cream

continued

¼ to ⅓ **cup dry sherry or sherry cooking wine**

2 **tablespoons chopped parsley**

7. Remove from the oven, uncover, and sprinkle with the parsley. Let stand for 10 to 15 minutes to allow the flavors to blend.

TIPS FROM OUR TEST KITCHEN: Ask your butcher to cut the pork loin and tenderize it for you. This can also be done with a meat mallet. The slices will resemble cube steak when tenderized. For a stronger sherry flavor, add 2 to 3 additional tablespoons.

Spareribs Polynesian

Francine McGinty, Spokane, Washington

Serves 8

"These are addictive and a crowd-pleaser. I serve them anytime family or friends get together, and they are always a hit."

1. Preheat the oven to 350°F.

2. Place the flour in the oven-browning bag, close the bag, and shake to coat the inside thoroughly. Add the ribs and secure the bag.

3. Bake for 1½ hours, following the manufacturer's directions for using the bag.

4. Combine the onion, soy sauce, vinegar, pineapple juice, sugar, oyster sauce, garlic, ginger, and cloves in a medium saucepan. Bring just to a boil over medium-high heat. Reduce the heat and simmer for 10 minutes.

5. At the end of the cooking time for the spareribs, open the bag and drain the fat. Carefully pour the sauce over the ribs and secure the bag. Bake for 30 minutes to 1 hour longer, until the ribs are tender. Serve with rice and broccoli.

1 tablespoon all-purpose flour

1 large oven-browning bag

4 to 5 pounds country-style spareribs, cut into serving-size pieces

1 medium onion, sliced and separated into rings

½ cup soy sauce

½ cup cider vinegar

½ cup pineapple juice

½ cup sugar

2 tablespoons oyster sauce

1 garlic clove, minced

¼ teaspoon ground ginger or 1 teaspoon grated fresh ginger

¼ teaspoon ground cloves

Cooked rice

Broccoli

TIPS FROM OUR TEST KITCHEN: To remove grease from the ribs, pour the liquid into a degreasing pitcher or pour the liquid into a quart-size zip-top plastic bag. Seal the bag and let stand for 3 to 5 minutes to allow the grease to rise to the top. Holding the bag over a bowl, snip one corner to release the liquid. Stop the flow when the grease comes near the opening. Discard the grease and add the liquid back to the oven bag.

Crabmeat au Gratin

Lillie Duhon, Port Neches, Texas

Serves 6

"*T*his dish is an all-time favorite of my husband, sons, and other family members. The first time I made it was Thanksgiving at my home—I should have doubled the recipe!"

½ cup (1 stick) butter

1 large onion, finely chopped

1 medium celery stalk, finely chopped

½ cup all-purpose flour

3 cups heavy cream or two 12-ounce
   cans evaporated milk

2 egg yolks

1 teaspoon salt

½ teaspoon cayenne pepper

¼ teaspoon black pepper

1 pound fresh crabmeat, picked over for
   shells and cartilage

2 cups shredded Cheddar

1. Preheat the oven to 375°F. Grease a 12×8-inch baking dish.

2. Melt the butter in a large skillet over medium heat. Add the onion and celery and cook until the onion is translucent, about 6 minutes, stirring frequently.

3. Add the flour and stir until well blended. Gradually add the cream, stirring constantly. Stir in the egg yolks, salt, cayenne, and black pepper and cook for 5 minutes, or until thickened.

4. Place the crabmeat in a medium bowl. Add the sauce and mix gently but thoroughly to blend. Spoon into the prepared pan. Sprinkle with the Cheddar.

5. Bake, uncovered, for 25 minutes, or until the cheese melts and begins to lightly brown.

Seafood Gumbo

Jaime Welch, Tilghman, Maryland

Serves 15 to 20

"I have prepared this Seafood Gumbo for a neighborhood Mardi Gras party."

1. Combine the onion, bell pepper, green onions, garlic, and parsley in a large bowl; mix well.

2. Heat the oil in a stockpot over medium heat. To prepare a roux, gradually add the flour and cook until medium brown, 15 to 20 minutes, stirring constantly. Use a flat spatula to scrape the bottom of the pot for even cooking. If the mixture begins to brown too quickly, reduce the heat to medium-low.

3. Add the onion mixture and cook over medium heat until the mixture begins to lightly brown, 4 to 5 minutes, stirring constantly. Stir in the tomatoes, kielbasa, okra, Creole seasoning, and beef broth. Increase the heat to high and bring to a boil, stirring frequently. Reduce the heat, and simmer, uncovered, for 1 hour, stirring occasionally.

4. Increase the heat to medium-high, add the shrimp, crabmeat, oysters with their liquor, and 1½ cups water.

1 large onion, chopped

1 large green bell pepper, chopped

6 green onions, chopped (white and green parts)

3 garlic cloves, minced

2 tablespoons minced parsley

¾ cup vegetable oil

¾ cup all-purpose flour

One 28-ounce can diced tomatoes, undrained

1 pound kielbasa, cut into ½-inch chunks, then chunks quartered

1 pound frozen cut okra, thawed

2 tablespoons Creole seasoning, such as Tony Chachère's Original Creole Seasoning, or to taste

2 quarts beef broth or 2 quarts water and 3 tablespoons beef bouillon granules

1 pound raw medium shrimp, peeled and deveined

continued

1 pound fresh crabmeat, picked over for shells and cartilage

1 pint shucked oysters, undrained

Hot pepper sauce

Cooked rice

Cook until the shrimp just turn pink and the oysters curl at the edges. Turn off the heat.

5. Add additional Creole seasoning, if desired. Serve with the hot pepper sauce over the hot cooked rice.

TIPS FROM OUR TEST KITCHEN: This dish is even better if refrigerated overnight before serving. Cool the gumbo before storing in the refrigerator. It freezes well. If you can't find the Creole seasoning locally, it is available from Tony Chachère's Web site, www.tonychachere.com.

Creamy Shrimp with Pasta

Vina Lewis, Fortuna, California

Serves 4 to 5

"I fixed this for my son and his new girlfriend, who were visiting from college. This is my lower fat version of Shrimp Fettuccine Alfredo. I added a salad, and all were happy."

1. Cook the pasta according to the package directions. Drain.

2. Heat the butter and olive oil in a large skillet over medium heat. When the butter is melted, add the shrimp and cook until opaque in the center, about 4 minutes, stirring frequently.

3. Add the garlic and cook for 30 seconds. Stir in the sour cream until well blended. Remove the skillet from the heat and add the cheese; mix gently. Add the French fried onions, if using.

4. Serve over the pasta with additional cheese.

8 ounces uncooked linguine or fettuccine

3 tablespoons butter

1 tablespoon olive oil

1 pound raw medium shrimp, peeled and deveined

8 garlic cloves, minced

1 cup light or regular sour cream

4 ounces Parmesan or Romano, grated, plus more for serving

½ to ¾ cup French's Original French Fried Onions, optional

Entrées   **155**

Shrimp Basil

Sandra Jordan, Graham, North Carolina

Serves 6 to 8

*"T*his healthful Mediterranean dish is my family's favorite. The vegetables are colorful and fresh, and the flavors are wonderful."

1 pound uncooked pasta, any variety

½ cup olive oil

1 garlic clove, minced

1 large bunch green onions, chopped (white and green parts)

3 large Roma tomatoes, coarsely chopped

¾ cup chopped basil, or to taste

2 tablespoons butter

1 pound raw medium shrimp, peeled and deveined

1 to 2 teaspoons sea salt, or to taste

1. Cook the pasta according to the package directions. Drain and set aside.

2. Heat 1 tablespoon of the olive oil in a large nonstick skillet over medium heat. Add the garlic and cook for 15 seconds, stirring constantly. Add the green onions, tomatoes, basil, butter, and the remaining olive oil.

3. When the butter melts, make a well in the center of the skillet. Add the shrimp and cook until they just turn pink, about 3 minutes. Do not stir. When the shrimp are cooked, stir one time and cook for 1 minute longer.

4. Arrange the pasta on a serving platter and spoon the shrimp and vegetables on top. Sprinkle with the salt; toss gently. Top with additional basil, if desired.

TIPS FROM OUR TEST KITCHEN: It is very important not to stir the mixture to make sure all the fresh flavors can be tasted. Stirring the mixture will break it down and dilute the flavors.

Shrimp Feast

Joe Bradford, Sea Island, Georgia

Serves 8 to 10

"*I* made this Shrimp Feast for a Christmas get-together, and it was enjoyed by all. I use a turkey fryer and a two-burner natural gas hot plate to do the cooking. It always turns out to be a great way to entertain my friends."

Combine 5 quarts water, the salt, beer, if using, and seafood seasoning in an 8-quart stockpot. Bring to a boil. Add the potatoes and onions; cook over high heat for 8 minutes. Add the sausage and cook over high heat for 5 minutes. Add the corn and boil for 7 minutes. Stir in the shrimp and cook for 4 minutes, or until opaque in the center. Drain well and ladle into large bowls. Serve with cocktail sauce, melted butter, or lemon wedges, if using.

2 tablespoons salt

One 12-ounce can beer, optional

½ cup seafood seasoning

8 medium red potatoes, cut into quarters (3 pounds)

2 large sweet onions, cut into wedges

2 pounds lean smoked sausage, cut into 2-inch lengths

8 ears fresh corn, cut in half

4 pounds raw, unpeeled large shrimp

Cocktail sauce, optional

Melted butter, optional

Lemon wedges, optional

TIPS FROM OUR TEST KITCHEN: Be sure to follow cooking times for each ingredient to ensure peak flavors and texture.

Eggplant Rolls

M. Vicianna Scaringi, Verona, Pennsylvania

Serves 6

One 2-pound eggplant

1 teaspoon salt

3 eggs, beaten

1 cup all-purpose flour

1 to 2 cups dry Italian bread crumbs

½ cup olive oil

One 26-ounce jar spaghetti sauce

FILLING

One 15-ounce container ricotta

6 ounces mozzarella, shredded

2 eggs

½ cup grated Parmesan or Romano

1 tablespoon finely chopped parsley or
    1 teaspoon dried basil

¼ teaspoon salt

⅛ teaspoon black pepper

1. To prepare the eggplant, cut lengthwise into 12 slices ⅛ to ¼ inch thick. Arrange the slices on a large sheet of foil. Sprinkle evenly with the salt and let stand for 30 minutes. Pat dry with paper towels.

2. Place the beaten eggs in one shallow bowl, the flour in a second bowl, and the bread crumbs in a third. Dip each eggplant slice in the eggs, the flour, and the bread crumbs. Remove to a plate to set the breading.

3. Heat ¼ cup of the olive oil in a large skillet over medium-high heat. Working in batches, fry the breaded eggplant until brown, about 1 minute on each side. Add the remaining oil if needed. Allow the oil to reach cooking temperature before adding additional eggplant. Drain on paper towels.

4. Preheat the oven to 350°F. Spray a 13×9-inch baking dish with nonstick cooking spray.

5. Spoon one-third of the spaghetti sauce over the bottom of the dish.

6. To prepare the filling, combine the ricotta, mozzarella, eggs, Parmesan, parsley, salt, and pepper in a medium bowl; mix well.

7. Place ⅓ cup of the filling in the center of an eggplant slice. Fold the ends toward the center and overlap to form a roll. Place seam side down in the prepared baking dish. Repeat with the remaining eggplant.

8. Pour the remaining spaghetti sauce evenly over the eggplant rolls.

9. To prepare the topping, sprinkle the mozzarella and Parmesan evenly over the top of the rolls.

10. Bake, uncovered, for 30 to 35 minutes, until the cheese is slightly golden.

TOPPING

4 ounces mozzarella, shredded (1 cup)

2 tablespoons grated Parmesan

Maria's Special Tomato Sauce

Maria Campanelli, New Bern, North Carolina

Serves 6

3 tablespoons olive oil

1 medium onion, finely chopped

2 garlic cloves, minced

Two 28-ounce cans peeled whole
    tomatoes, undrained

2 tablespoons tomato paste

1 teaspoon dried Italian seasoning

1 teaspoon sea salt

1 pound uncooked ziti

5 or 6 basil leaves, chopped

1. Heat the olive oil in a large saucepan over medium heat. Add the onion and cook for 3 minutes, stirring frequently. Add the garlic and cook for 30 seconds, stirring constantly. Remove from the heat and set aside.

2. Working in two batches, place the tomatoes in a blender and process for 30 seconds or until smooth. Add the tomato mixture to the onion mixture. Stir in the tomato paste, Italian seasoning, and salt. Bring the mixture to a boil, reduce the heat, and simmer, uncovered, for 1½ hours, stirring occasionally.

3. Cook the pasta according to the package directions; drain well. Serve with the sauce and sprinkle with the basil.

TIPS FROM OUR TEST KITCHEN: Don't omit the fresh basil.

Onion Quiche

Jeannie Hutchins, Newport, Washington

Serves 4 to 6

"*T*his is a wonderful quiche. Our family loves this quiche on holidays and during the winter when it is cold outside. It is great with the two kinds of onions—caramelized on the bottom and fried on top."

1. Preheat the oven to 375°F.

2. Melt the butter in a large skillet over medium heat. Add the onions and cook for 20 minutes, until caramelized, stirring frequently. Add the sugar and cream sherry and cook until the onions are very soft and golden, about 4 minutes, stirring frequently. The onions will cook down considerably. Remove the onions to a dinner plate and place in the freezer for 3 to 5 minutes to cool quickly.

3. Whisk the eggs, half-and-half, and nutmeg in a bowl until well blended. Place the piecrust on a baking sheet.

4. Remove the caramelized onions from the freezer and arrange them in the bottom of the pie shell. Top with the shredded Swiss cheese. Sprinkle evenly with the French fried onions and pour the egg mixture over all.

5. Bake on the middle rack of the oven for 30 minutes, or until a knife inserted in the center comes out clean. Serve hot or at room temperature.

3 tablespoons butter

2 large white onions, thinly sliced

1 tablespoon sugar

2 tablespoons cream sherry

2 eggs

1 cup half-and-half

½ teaspoon freshly grated nutmeg

One 9-inch unbaked piecrust

2 cups shredded Swiss cheese

1 cup French's Original French Fried Onions

Spinach Pie

Lois Carlson, Palisade, Minnesota

Serves 4 to 6

"*I* enjoy inviting people over after church. With family and friends, there are usually at least ten people gathered around our large country table. My Spinach Pie has been quite a hit, so I keep making it."

One 10-ounce package frozen chopped
  spinach, thawed and squeezed dry
1 medium onion, coarsely chopped
1 cup shredded Cheddar
One 3-ounce package cream cheese,
  softened
3 eggs
¼ cup milk
1 to 2 garlic cloves
½ teaspoon salt
One 9-inch unbaked piecrust
2 tablespoons grated Parmesan
1 medium tomato, thinly sliced
½ to ¾ cup French's Original French
  Fried Onions

1. Preheat the oven to 350°F.

2. Combine the spinach, onion, Cheddar, cream cheese, eggs, milk, garlic, and salt in a blender or food processor and process until well blended. Pour into the piecrust.

3. Sprinkle the Parmesan over the filling and top with the tomato slices. Sprinkle the French fried onions evenly over the tomatoes.

4. Bake for 45 to 55 minutes, until a knife inserted in the center comes out clean.

Tomato Pie

Carole VanCleave, Concord, North Carolina

Serves 4 to 6

"This is especially good in the summer with fresh garden tomatoes."

1. Preheat the oven to 400°F. Bake the piecrust for 10 to 12 minutes, until golden. Cool on a wire rack.

2. Reduce the oven temperature to 350°F. Sprinkle half of the mozzarella on the bottom of the cooled piecrust. Top with the tomato slices and arrange the onion slices evenly over the tomatoes.

3. Combine the salad dressing, remaining mozzarella, the basil, salt, and pepper in a small bowl; mix well. Spoon over the tomatoes and onions.

4. Bake for 40 to 45 minutes, until bubbly and golden brown.

One 9-inch unbaked piecrust

1½ cups shredded mozzarella

3 to 4 medium tomatoes, thinly sliced

⅓ cup thinly sliced Vidalia onion

½ cup Caesar salad dressing

½ teaspoon dried basil, or to taste

½ teaspoon salt

⅛ teaspoon black pepper, or to taste

Desserts

"What's for dessert?" It's not only children, but adults, too, who want to know which treat awaits them at the end of a scrumptious meal. Often a prized recipe for cookies, cakes, or pies satisfies that persistent sweet tooth.

Rich chocolate and orange—Michelle Gauer's Fudge Cappuccino Orange Torte has it all. Gauer, of Spicer, Minnesota, enjoys the pairing of flavors so much that she makes it on her birthday and gives everyone else a treat. The decadent torte took the Grand Prize in *American Profile* magazine's Hometown Get-Togethers Recipe Contest.

Millie DuBovy of Lady Lake, Florida, has many years' experience baking her Midnight Biscotti—fifty to be exact! She estimates she has served her tasty treat to at least a thousand people at family get-togethers, but she'll also make the biscotti "just for me," she admits. DuBovy is eighty-seven.

Another family legacy is carried on whenever a batch of Grandma's Buttermilk Brownie Cake comes out of Connie Mrachek's oven in Charles City, Iowa. There's no doubt the recipe is a winner—it's been a family favorite for five generations, Mrachek says.

Diane's Absolutely Awesome Chocolate Cake is fancy enough to serve at a birthday party, but easy—and foolproof—for a novice baker, says Diane McCrory of Trinity, Texas. McCrory says her yummy cake is a hit with both adults and kids—including her eight grandchildren.

Barbara Chapman of Casper, Wyoming, has solved the problem of satisfying both cake and pie lovers when it's time to prepare a dessert. Her solution is Reunion Cake and Pie, which made its debut at her family's reunions at Fort Robinson, Nebraska. Family members come from forty states for the event, and she must travel as well to get there. Reunion Cake and Pie can be made ahead, travels well, and freezes well, Chapman says, making it a winner all around.

Walnut Roca Bars

Stephanie Burkett, Chico, California

Makes 2 dozen bars

"Whether I have prepared these bars for family, church, or community activities, I am often told that 'these cookies are to die for.'"

1. Preheat the oven to 350°F. Line a 13×9-inch baking pan with foil, leaving a 2-inch overhang. Coat the foil with nonstick cooking spray.

2. To prepare the crust, combine the butter, flour, and brown sugar in a bowl. Mix with a pastry blender until crumbly. Press into the prepared pan.

3. To prepare the middle layer, combine the butter and brown sugar in a small saucepan. Bring to a boil and boil for 2 minutes, stirring constantly. Pour over the crust and bake for 15 to 18 minutes, until the crust is golden brown. Remove from the oven.

4. To prepare the topping, sprinkle the walnuts, chocolate chips, and Heath chips evenly over the top of the bars. Press gently with the back of a spoon. Cool in the pan on a wire rack until the chocolate is set.

5. To serve, lift the foil overhang to remove the entire dessert from the pan. Cut into 2-inch squares. Store in an airtight container.

CRUST

½ cup (1 stick) butter
1½ cups all-purpose flour
1 cup packed light brown sugar

MIDDLE LAYER

½ cup (1 stick) butter
⅓ cup packed light brown sugar

TOPPING

1 cup finely chopped walnuts
1 cup semisweet chocolate chips
1 cup Heath chips

Glazed Apple Bars

Donna Roberts, Shumway, Illinois

Makes 2 dozen bars

"This is a melt-in-your-mouth recipe that makes a lot of servings. It has a spicy, nutty taste that everyone loves."

BARS

½ cup (1 stick) butter or margarine, softened
1⅓ cups packed light brown sugar
½ teaspoon salt
½ teaspoon ground nutmeg
1 teaspoon ground cinnamon
1 teaspoon ground cloves
1 egg
2 cups all-purpose flour
1 teaspoon baking soda
1 medium chopped red apple, such as Gala, peeled if desired
1 cup raisins
1 cup chopped pecans
¼ cup milk

GLAZE

1½ cups confectioners' sugar
2½ tablespoons warm milk
1 tablespoon butter or margarine, softened
¼ teaspoon vanilla extract
⅛ teaspoon salt

1. Preheat the oven to 400°F. Lightly grease a 15×10-inch jelly roll pan.

2. To prepare the bars, cream the butter and brown sugar with a mixer at medium-high speed. Add the salt, nutmeg, cinnamon, cloves, and egg; beat until well blended.

3. Combine 1 cup of the flour and the baking soda in a bowl; add to the butter mixture. Stir in the apple, raisins, and pecans by hand. Add the milk and the remaining flour; mix well. Spread in the prepared pan. Bake for 10 to 14 minutes, until light brown. Cool for 10 minutes.

4. To prepare the glaze, combine the confectioners' sugar, milk, butter, vanilla, and salt in a bowl; mix well. Spread the glaze over the cooled bars and cut into serving pieces.

Midnight Biscotti

Millie DuBovy, Lady Lake, Florida

Makes 28 to 32 biscotti

"I have been making this biscotti for approximately fifty years. I've served it to at least a thousand people at get-togethers, family gatherings, and just for me. It has never failed to be a hit. I'm eighty-seven years old."

1. Preheat the oven to 350°F. Grease two baking sheets.

2. To prepare the biscotti, combine the eggs, granulated sugar, oil, and almond extract in a large bowl. Beat well with a mixer at medium speed.

3. Stir together 3¾ cups of the flour, the cocoa powder, baking powder, and salt in a separate bowl. Add to the egg mixture. Beat at low speed until the ingredients are combined. Increase the speed to medium and mix until well blended. Stir in the walnuts.

4. If the batter is too wet, add 1 to 2 tablespoons flour, just enough to shape the dough easily. With floured hands, quickly shape into 12×2-inch rolls and place on the prepared pans.

5. Bake for 30 minutes. Remove from the oven and cool slightly. Slice each roll diagonally into ¾-inch-thick slices.

6. Reduce the oven temperature to 200°F. Stand the biscotti upright on their long edge on the baking sheets and return to the oven. Bake for 30 minutes, or until very dry. Remove to wire racks to cool completely.

7. To prepare the icing, if using, combine the confectioners' sugar, almond extract, and milk in a bowl; mix well. Spread on top of the cooled biscotti.

BISCOTTI

3 eggs

1 cup granulated sugar

½ cup vegetable oil

1 tablespoon almond or orange extract

3 ¾ cups plus 1 to 2 tablespoons all-purpose flour

¼ cup dark cocoa powder

1¼ teaspoons baking powder

¼ teaspoon salt

½ cup chopped walnuts or almonds

ICING (OPTIONAL)

1½ cups confectioners' sugar

¼ teaspoon almond extract

2 teaspoons milk, or more as needed

Dried Fruit Pinwheels for a Crowd

Beth Jacobson, Green Spring, West Virginia

Makes about 8 dozen pinwheels

"These are special holiday cookies that I give to friends and have on hand at home for visitors. They also freeze well."

DOUGH

1¼ cups vegetable shortening

2½ cups granulated sugar

1¼ cups plus 2 to 3 tablespoons butter-milk or sour milk

2½ teaspoons vanilla extract

8½ to 8¾ cups all-purpose flour

2½ teaspoons baking soda

5 teaspoons baking powder

FILLING

8 cups dried fruit (any combination of dried cherries, cranberries, chopped pitted dates, raisins, golden raisins, chopped apricots)

2½ cups granulated sugar

6 tablespoons all-purpose flour

1 teaspoon ground cinnamon

1 teaspoon ground cardamom

1 teaspoon ground nutmeg

1 teaspoon ground allspice

1 teaspoon ground cloves

1. To prepare the dough, cream the shortening and granulated sugar with a mixer at medium speed. Reduce the speed to low and add 1¼ cups of the buttermilk and the vanilla. Sift together the flour, baking soda, and baking powder. Add gradually to the creamed mixture and beat at low speed until well blended. If the dough is dry, add 2 to 3 tablespoons additional buttermilk. Divide the dough into 4 equal parts, wrap in plastic wrap, and refrigerate for at least 30 minutes.

2. To prepare the filling, combine the dried fruit, granulated sugar, 2½ cups water, the flour, and spices in a Dutch oven. Bring to a boil over medium-high heat, stirring frequently to keep the filling from scorching on the bottom. Cook to 200°F on a candy thermometer. Cool completely and divide into 4 equal portions.

3. Preheat the oven to 375°F. Grease several baking sheets or line with parchment paper.

4. Remove 1 ball of dough from the refrigerator. Dust the countertop and a rolling pin with confectioners' sugar and roll the dough into a ¼-inch-thick rectangle. Spread 1 portion of the filling on the rectangle. Sprinkle with ½ cup of the almonds and 2 tablespoons of the raw sugar.

5. Starting with the long end, roll up jelly roll fashion and slice into ½-inch pieces. Place on the prepared baking sheets. Bake for about 15 minutes, or until lightly browned. Repeat with the remaining dough, filling, and topping.

Confectioners' sugar

2 cups slivered almonds, toasted

½ cup turbinado sugar (raw sugar)

TIPS FROM OUR TEST KITCHEN: To make slicing the pinwheels easier, clean and dry the knife frequently. This recipe makes enough pinwheels to feed an army—and then some. Refrigerate the rolls for 2 to 3 days before slicing and baking, if desired.

Fudge-Filled Bars

Delilah E. Schwartz, Berne, Indiana

Makes 2 to 3 dozen bars

"This is a good treat when my sisters get together."

CRUST

2 cups quick-cooking oats

1½ cups all-purpose flour

1 cup packed light brown sugar

1 cup (2 sticks) butter or margarine, melted

1 cup chopped pecans

TOPPING

One 14-ounce can sweetened condensed milk

1 cup semisweet chocolate chips

2 tablespoons vegetable shortening

1 cup candy-coated pieces, such as M&M's

1. Preheat the oven to 350°F. Grease a 13×9-inch baking pan.

2. To prepare the bars, combine the oats, flour, and brown sugar in a bowl. Add the melted butter and mix until crumbly. Stir in the pecans. Set aside 1½ cups of the crumb mixture. Press the remaining mixture into the bottom of the prepared pan.

3. To prepare the topping, combine the condensed milk, chocolate chips, and shortening in a medium saucepan over low heat. Cook and stir until the chips are melted. Spread over the crust and top with the reserved crumb mixture.

4. Sprinkle the M&M's over the top. Bake for 20 to 25 minutes, until the edges are golden brown. Cool and slice into bars.

No-Bake Peanut Butter Logs

Janice Cooper, Argos, Indiana

Makes 40 logs

"I make these logs every Christmas. They are a tradition, along with several other cookie recipes. Everyone loves them—even people who don't like nuts."

1. Combine the peanut butter and margarine in a mixing bowl. Beat until smooth with a mixer at medium speed. Beat in the confectioners' sugar. Stir in the cereal with a wooden spoon.

2. Using 1 level tablespoon of dough for each log, shape the dough into 2½-inch-long logs. Roll the logs in the peanuts and place on wax paper.

3. Combine the chocolate chips and shortening in a microwave-safe bowl. Heat in the microwave until melted. Drizzle the chocolate mixture over the logs and top with a few chopped peanuts. Let stand until set. Store in an airtight container.

1 cup creamy peanut butter

¼ cup (½ stick) margarine, softened

1½ cups confectioners' sugar

3 cups crispy rice cereal

1 cup chopped peanuts

One 6-ounce package semisweet chocolate chips

2 tablespoons vegetable shortening

Pecan Pie Bars

Shirley Lockwood, Constantine, Michigan

Makes 3 dozen bars

"*T*hese bars are much easier to make than pecan pie. They serve more people, and you can serve smaller portions—they are very rich."

BARS

3 cups all-purpose flour

¾ cup granulated sugar

½ teaspoon salt

½ cup (1 stick) butter (no substitutes)

FILLING

4 eggs

1 cup granulated sugar

½ cup packed light brown sugar

1½ cups light or dark corn syrup

1½ teaspoons vanilla extract

2½ cups chopped pecans

1. Preheat the oven to 350°F. Lightly grease a 13×9-inch baking pan.

2. To prepare the bars, combine the flour, granulated sugar, salt, and butter in a food processor. Pulse two or three times until the mixture is crumbly. Press on the bottom of the prepared pan. Bake for 18 to 22 minutes, until the edges of the crust begin to brown. Cool completely.

3. To prepare the filling, combine the eggs, granulated sugar, brown sugar, corn syrup, and vanilla in a large bowl. Mix until well blended with a mixer at low speed. Stir in the pecans and pour over the cooled crust. Bake for 25 to 35 minutes, until the center is almost set. Cool and cut into bars.

Apple Cake

Debra Paszko, Effort, Pennsylvania

Serves 12 to 16

"*T*his recipe is a favorite at company picnics. My fellow employees really enjoy it, and many of the ladies ask me to bake this for them to take to their family functions."

1. Preheat the oven to 450°F. Grease and flour a 13×9-inch metal cake pan.

2. Combine ½ cup of the sugar, the cinnamon, and walnuts in a small bowl; mix well.

3. For the batter, mix the flour, remaining 2 cups sugar, the eggs, orange juice, oil, baking powder, and vanilla in a large bowl. Stir with a wooden spoon.

4. Pour half of the batter into the prepared pan. Place half of the apples on top of the batter and sprinkle with half of the cinnamon mixture. Repeat with the remaining batter, apples, and cinnamon mixture.

5. Bake for 15 minutes. Reduce the oven temperature to 350°F and bake for 40 minutes longer, or until the cake is golden brown and beginning to pull away from the sides of the pan.

2½ cups sugar

2 teaspoons ground cinnamon

½ cup chopped walnuts

3 cups all-purpose flour

4 eggs

½ cup orange juice

1 cup vegetable oil

1 tablespoon baking powder

2 teaspoons vanilla extract

6 or 7 apples, such as Gala, peeled and chopped

Blackberry Cake

Elsie Cumpton, Worthington, Kentucky

Serves 12

"*T*his is a good, moist cake to send to people in the armed services. I sent this Blackberry Cake to my husband, who was stationed in Germany with the U.S. Army in the 1950s."

1 cup vegetable shortening

3 eggs

2 cups sugar

1 cup blackberries, fresh or frozen

1 cup buttermilk

1 teaspoon baking soda

3 cups all-purpose flour

1 teaspoon salt

1 teaspoon ground nutmeg

1 teaspoon ground cinnamon

1 teaspoon ground cloves

1. Preheat the oven to 350°F. Grease and flour two 9-inch round cake pans.

2. Cream the shortening, eggs, and sugar with a mixer at medium speed. Stir in the blackberries.

3. Mix the buttermilk and baking soda in a small bowl. Combine the flour, salt, nutmeg, cinnamon, and cloves in a large bowl; mix well.

4. Add the buttermilk mixture and the flour mixture alternately to the creamed blackberry mixture; beat well. Pour into the prepared cake pans.

5. Bake for 30 to 40 minutes, until a wooden pick inserted in the center comes out almost clean. Do not overbake. Cool on a wire rack.

Grandma's Buttermilk Brownie Cake

Connie Mrachek, Charles City, Iowa

Serves 36

"*T*his recipe has been a family favorite for five generations. My grandmother, Ruthie Rice, has passed away, but her brownie cake is still a family favorite at all of our gatherings."

1. Preheat the oven to 400°F. Grease one 15×10-inch baking pan.

2. To prepare the cake, combine the granulated sugar, flour, and cocoa in a large bowl; mix well.

3. Combine 1 cup water with the oil and butter in a medium saucepan. Bring to a boil and add to the flour mixture; mix well. Add the buttermilk, baking soda, eggs, and vanilla. Beat well by hand and pour into the prepared pan. Bake for 20 to 25 minutes, until a wooden pick inserted in the center comes out almost clean. Cool completely on a wire rack.

4. To prepare the frosting, bring the butter, cocoa, and buttermilk to a boil in a large saucepan. Remove from the heat. Gradually beat in the confectioners' sugar and vanilla with a mixer at low speed. Spread evenly over the cooled cake.

CAKE

2 cups granulated sugar

2 cups all-purpose flour

¼ cup cocoa powder

½ cup vegetable oil

½ cup (1 stick) butter or margarine

½ cup buttermilk

1 teaspoon baking soda

2 eggs, lightly beaten

1 teaspoon vanilla extract

FROSTING

½ cup (1 stick) butter or margarine

¼ cup cocoa powder

⅓ cup buttermilk

One 1-pound box confectioners' sugar

1 teaspoon vanilla extract

Honey-Spiced Chai Bundt Cake

Wendy Nickel, Kiester, Minnesota

Serves 12

"Moist and flavorful, this cake is always a hit at my family reunions, local bake sales, and at school for my fellow staff members."

CAKE

2½ cups all-purpose flour

1½ cups packed light brown sugar

2 teaspoons baking soda

½ teaspoon salt

1¾ cups hot chai tea, cooled

½ cup buttermilk

½ cup honey

½ cup (1 stick) butter, melted and
    slightly cooled

2 eggs

1 egg yolk

ICING

One 16-ounce container cream cheese
    frosting

½ cup chopped pecans, toasted,
    if desired

1. Preheat the oven to 350°F. Spray a 10-cup Bundt pan with nonstick cooking spray.

2. To prepare the cake, combine the flour, brown sugar, baking soda, salt, tea, buttermilk, honey, butter, eggs, and egg yolk in a large bowl. Beat with a mixer at low speed for 1 minute, or until just blended, scraping the sides of the bowl frequently.

3. Pour the batter into the prepared pan. Bake for 45 to 50 minutes, until a wooden pick inserted in the center comes out clean. Remove to a wire rack to cool completely. Remove from the pan.

4. To prepare the icing, remove the lid from the frosting and heat in the microwave until the frosting is slightly melted. Drizzle over the cooled cake and garnish with the pecans, if using.

Cherry Dump Cake

Eleanor Joyner, Loveland, Colorado

Serves 16

"I make Cherry Dump Cake for church groups and family. It's good anytime and so easy to make."

1. Preheat the oven to 350°F.

2. Pour the peaches and their syrup and the drained pineapple into a 13×9-inch cake pan. Top with the cherry pie filling. Sprinkle the dry cake mix over the pie filling and pour the melted butter over the top. Sprinkle with the walnuts.

3. Bake for 45 to 55 minutes, until golden brown. Cool on a wire rack for at least 30 minutes until the cake is at room temperature.

One 15-ounce can peach slices in light
   syrup, undrained
One 20-ounce can pineapple chunks
   packed in juice, drained
Two 21-ounce cans cherry pie filling,
   preferably no-sugar-added variety
One 18-ounce package yellow cake mix
1 cup (2 sticks) butter, melted
½ cup chopped walnuts or pecans

Chocolate Snowball Cake

Connie Turner, Crossville, Tennessee

Serves 12 to 16

*"E*veryone gave me rave reviews when I created this Chocolate Snowball Cake to share with friends and coworkers at my sometimes hectic and chaotic office. They are my taste testers, and I am always trying new twists to my cakes and other desserts."

CAKE

½ cup shredded sweetened coconut

One 18-ounce package chocolate fudge
    cake mix

3 eggs

½ cup vegetable oil

½ cup semisweet chocolate chips

1 tablespoon chocolate syrup, optional

4 fudge cookies with marshmallow and
    coconut, such as Little Debbie
    Coconut Puffs, crumbled

½ cup miniature marshmallows

FROSTING

Four 1-ounce chocolate-coated
    almond-coconut candy bars, such as
    Almond Joy

One 16-ounce container vanilla frosting

1 teaspoon almond extract

1 teaspoon brewed coffee or water

1. Preheat the oven to 350°F. Grease a 13×9-inch baking pan.

2. To prepare the cake, sprinkle the bottom of the prepared pan with the coconut. Combine the cake mix, eggs, 1⅓ cups water, and the oil in a bowl, according to the package directions; mix well.

3. Stir in the chocolate chips, syrup, if using, the cookies, and marshmallows; mix well. Pour the batter into the prepared pan. Bake as directed for the cake mix, about 35 minutes, or until a wooden pick inserted in the center comes out clean. Cool completely on a wire rack.

4. To prepare the frosting, melt the candy bars in a microwave-safe bowl. Remove from the microwave and cool to lukewarm. Combine the candy with the frosting, almond extract, and coffee in a bowl; mix well. Spread over the cooled cake.

Diane's Absolutely Awesome Chocolate Cake

Diane McCrory, Trinity, Texas

"*M*y chocolate cake is always a hit for adults and kids alike—I have eight grandchildren. It is fancy enough for a birthday party or easy and failproof for a novice baker."

1. Preheat the oven to 350°F. Grease a 13×9-inch baking dish.

2. To prepare the cake, combine the butter and granulated sugar in a large bowl. Using an electric mixer at medium-high speed, beat until fluffy, about 2 minutes.

3. Add the eggs, vanilla, and melted chocolate; beat until blended. Combine the flour, baking powder, baking soda, and salt in a separate bowl; mix well.

4. Reduce the mixer speed to low. Add the flour mixture to the egg mixture alternately with the milk, beginning and ending with the flour mixture. Mix well.

5. To prepare the filling, combine the cream cheese, butter, granulated sugar, and cornstarch in a large bowl. Beat until smooth with a mixer at medium speed. Reduce the mixer speed to low and add the

CAKE

½ cup (1 stick) butter, softened

2 cups granulated sugar

2 eggs

1 teaspoon vanilla extract

4 ounces unsweetened baking chocolate, melted

2 cups all-purpose flour

1 teaspoon baking powder

½ teaspoon baking soda

1 teaspoon salt

1⅓ cups milk

FILLING

Two 8-ounce packages cream cheese, softened

¼ cup (½ stick) butter, softened

½ cup granulated sugar

2 tablespoons cornstarch

2 eggs

¼ cup milk

1 teaspoon vanilla extract

continued

½ cup (1 stick) butter

½ cup milk

4 ounces unsweetened baking chocolate

2 teaspoons vanilla extract

One 1-pound package confectioners' sugar

eggs, milk, and vanilla; beat until just blended. Increase the mixer speed to medium and blend until smooth.

6. To assemble the cake, spread half of the batter in the prepared pan. Carefully spoon the filling on top. Spread the remaining cake batter on top of the filling.

7. Bake for 55 to 65 minutes, until a wooden pick inserted in the center comes out almost clean. Remove to a wire rack to cool completely.

8. To prepare the icing, heat the butter and milk in a large saucepan over medium-high heat. Bring just to a boil and remove from the heat immediately. Whisk in the chocolate and vanilla, stirring until the chocolate is melted.

9. Blend in the confectioners' sugar with a hand-held mixer at high speed until the icing is creamy. Pour over the cooled cake and spread evenly. Refrigerate until serving time.

TIPS FROM OUR TEST KITCHEN: For best results, use high-quality chocolate.

Old-Fashioned Oatmeal Cake with Broiled Topping

Denise Bradley, Bowling Green, Kentucky

Serves 12 to 16

"This recipe has been in my family for many years. I often bake it for my brother's birthday, because it's his favorite cake. I also have taken this cake to work and church functions because everyone seems to enjoy it."

1. Preheat the oven to 350°F. Grease and flour a 13×9-inch cake pan.

2. To prepare the cake, pour 1¼ cups boiling water over the oats in a bowl. Let stand for 20 minutes. Cream the butter, granulated sugar, and brown sugar with a mixer. Add the oats; mix well. Add the eggs and vanilla; mix well.

3. Sift together the flour, baking soda, salt, and cinnamon. Add to the oats mixture; mix well. Pour into the prepared pan. Bake for 30 to 35 minutes, until browned.

4. Preheat the broiler.

5. To prepare the topping, combine the butter, cream, brown sugar, and coconut in a medium bowl; mix well. Spread evenly over the warm cake. Place the cake under the broiler 2 inches from the heat source. Broil until lightly browned, 1 to 1½ minutes. Cool on a wire rack.

CAKE

1 cup old-fashioned oats

½ cup (1 stick) butter, softened

1 cup granulated sugar

1 cup packed light brown sugar

2 eggs

1 teaspoon vanilla extract

1⅓ cups all-purpose flour

1 teaspoon baking soda

½ teaspoon salt

1 teaspoon ground cinnamon

TOPPING

¼ cup (½ stick) butter, softened

¼ cup heavy cream

1 cup packed light brown sugar

1 cup shredded sweetened coconut

Old-Fashioned Orange Layer Cake

Pauline Brown, Chinquapin, North Carolina

Serves 12 to 16

"This delicious recipe is probably over seventy-five years old. My aunt used to bake this cake for Christmas and my mother's birthday dinner."

CAKE

2 cups granulated sugar

1 cup (2 sticks) butter, softened

5 eggs, at room temperature

1 tablespoon grated orange zest

½ cup orange juice

2½ cups self-rising flour

1 cup milk

ICING

¼ cup (½ stick) butter, softened

1 tablespoon grated orange zest

⅓ cup freshly squeezed orange juice

One 1-pound package confectioners' sugar

1. Preheat the oven to 350°F. Grease and flour two 9-inch round cake pans.

2. To prepare the cake, combine the granulated sugar and butter in a large bowl; cream well with a mixer at medium-high speed. Add the eggs and orange zest; blend well.

3. Reduce the speed to low and beat in the orange juice. Add the flour alternately with the milk; beat well. Pour into the prepared pans.

4. Bake for 22 to 25 minutes, until a wooden pick inserted in the center comes out clean. Cool in the pans for 15 minutes. Remove from the pans and cool completely on wire racks.

5. To prepare the icing, combine the butter, orange zest, orange juice, and half of the confectioners' sugar in a large bowl. Using mixer at low speed, beat until well blended. Gradually beat in the remaining sugar until smooth.

6. When the cake has cooled, place one layer on a decorative plate. Spread about 3/4 cup of the icing on the top. Place the second layer on top. Spread the icing in a thin layer over the top and sides of the cake.

Orange Pumpkin Sheet Cake

Stacey Bornemann, Center, North Dakota

Serves 12 to 16

"I bake this cake for family birthdays. I have six brothers and sisters, and we usually get together at my parents' house. I have also taken this cake to work to share with my coworkers."

1. Preheat the oven to 350°F. Grease a 13×9-inch pan.

2. To prepare the cake, combine the cake mix, pudding mix, cinnamon, eggs, orange juice concentrate, oil, and pumpkin in a large bowl; mix well. Pour the batter into the prepared pan.

3. Bake for 30 to 35 minutes, until a wooden pick inserted in the center comes out clean. Cool completely in the pan on a wire rack.

4. To prepare the frosting, beat the cream cheese and butter with a mixer at low speed until well blended. Add the confectioners' sugar and orange juice concentrate alternately to the cream cheese mixture. Mix until smooth.

5. Spread the frosting evenly over the cooled cake.

CAKE

One 18-ounce package white cake mix

One 3-ounce package instant vanilla pudding mix

2 teaspoons ground cinnamon

4 eggs

⅔ cup frozen orange juice concentrate

½ cup vegetable oil

2 cups puréed pumpkin

FROSTING

One 8-ounce package cream cheese, softened

½ cup (1 stick) butter, softened

3 cups confectioners' sugar

1 to 2 tablespoons frozen orange juice concentrate

TIPS FROM OUR TEST KITCHEN: Applesauce may be substituted for the oil in the cake, if desired.

Pear Rum Cake with Chocolate Topping

Nancy Piazza, Lucerne, California

Serves 12

"*T*his cake was taken to the Pear Festival BBQ and won best of show. I have also served it many times to our dinner guests. My husband enjoys it very much."

CAKE

One 18-ounce package yellow cake mix

One 3-ounce package vanilla instant pudding mix

4 eggs

½ cup vegetable oil

½ cup 80-proof rum

3 large pears, peeled, cored, and quartered

RUM GLAZE

½ cup (1 stick) butter or margarine

1 cup sugar

½ cup 80-proof rum

TOPPING

6 ounces semisweet chocolate chips

2 tablespoons milk

1 tablespoon butter

1. Preheat the oven to 350°F. Grease and flour a 10-inch Bundt pan.

2. To prepare the cake, combine the cake mix, pudding mix, eggs, oil, rum, and ½ cup cold water in a large bowl. Mix until just blended with a mixer at low speed. Increase the speed to medium and beat for 2 minutes, scraping the side of the bowl occasionally. Pour into the prepared pan. Arrange the 8 slices from two of the pears on top so that each fluted section of the pan has a slice.

3. Bake for 45 to 50 minutes, until a wooden pick inserted in the center comes out clean. Cool in the pan for 10 minutes. Invert onto a serving plate.

4. To prepare the glaze, melt the butter in a medium saucepan over medium-low heat. Stir in ¼ cup water and the sugar. Bring to a simmer and cook for 5 minutes. Remove from the heat and add the rum.

5. Using a fork, prick the top of the cake and drizzle half of the glaze over the top. Chop the remaining pear and add to the glaze in the saucepan. Cook for 5 minutes. Spoon the remaining glaze and pears over the cake.

6. To prepare the topping, combine the chocolate chips, milk, and butter in a small saucepan over low heat. Heat until the chocolate chips are melted, stirring frequently. Drizzle over the cake. Garnish with chopped nuts, maraschino cherries, and whipped cream, if using.

2 tablespoons finely chopped nuts, optional
Maraschino cherries, optional
Whipped cream, optional

Reunion Cake and Pie

Barbara Chapman, Casper, Wyoming

"*I* first served this cake/pie combination at our semiannual family reunion at Fort Robinson, Nebraska. Our family has spread to forty states! This dessert can be made ahead, travels well, and freezes well. It also solves the problem of some people wanting pie and some wanting cake."

BOTTOM LAYER

1 cup dark corn syrup

2 tablespoons butter, melted

1 cup chopped pecans

⅔ cup packed light brown sugar

3 eggs, beaten

1 teaspoon vanilla extract

⅛ teaspoon salt

TOP LAYER

¼ cup (½ stick) butter, softened

½ cup granulated sugar

1 egg

2 teaspoons vanilla extract

1 cup all-purpose flour

¾ teaspoon baking powder

¼ teaspoon salt

¼ cup milk

Whipped cream, optional

Pecans, optional

1. Preheat the oven to 400°F. Grease a 9- or 10-inch round cake pan.

2. To prepare the bottom layer, combine the corn syrup, butter, pecans, brown sugar, eggs, vanilla, and salt in a medium bowl. Stir with a spoon until well blended.

3. Pour into the prepared pan. Bake for 15 minutes. Remove from the oven. Reduce the oven temperature to 375°F.

4. To prepare the top layer, combine the butter and granulated sugar in a medium bowl. Beat until light and creamy with a mixer at medium speed. Beat in the egg and add the vanilla.

5. Combine the flour, baking powder, and salt in a separate bowl; mix well. Gradually fold the flour mixture into the creamed mixture alternately with the milk; mix well. Pour over the baked bottom layer.

6. Bake for 20 minutes, or until golden around the edges and a wooden pick inserted in the center comes out clean. Immediately run a knife around the edge of the pan and invert onto a wire rack. Scrape any remaining pecan mixture onto the cake and smooth with the back of a spoon. Cool completely. Serve with a dollop of whipped cream and a few pecans, if using.

Cheesecake with a Lemon Twist

Diane Nemitz, Ludington, Michigan

Serves 24

"*M*y mother always brought this cake to family gatherings, potlucks, or card parties. It has been handed down to me, and I have handed it down to my daughter, who makes it for her guests as well. I love lemon, so I added the lemon curd."

1. Preheat the oven to 325°F.

2. To prepare the crust, combine the graham cracker crumbs and the melted butter in a bowl; mix well. Press into the bottom of a glass 13×9-inch baking dish. Bake for 5 minutes; remove from the oven.

3. To prepare the filling, place the cream cheese in a large bowl. Beat until smooth with a mixer at medium-high speed. Add the eggs, one at a time, followed by the sugar, vanilla, and lemon zest. Pour over the crust.

4. Bake for 1 hour, or until set. Remove from the oven and let stand. Maintain the oven temperature.

5. To prepare the topping, remove the lid from the jar of lemon curd. Heat in the microwave on high for 1 minute. Quickly spread over the cheesecake.

6. Combine the sour cream, sugar, and vanilla in a medium bowl; mix well. Spoon dollops on top of the lemon curd. Using the back of a spoon, spread carefully to cover the top. Return the cheesecake to the oven and bake for 15 minutes. Cool completely on a wire rack and then refrigerate until well chilled.

CRUST

1 cup graham cracker crumbs
¼ cup (½ stick) butter, melted

FILLING

Four 8-ounce packages cream cheese, softened
6 eggs
1 cup sugar
1 teaspoon vanilla extract
Grated zest of 1 lemon

TOPPING

One 10-ounce jar lemon curd
2 cups sour cream
½ cup sugar
1 teaspoon vanilla extract

Chocolate Cheesecake

Roseanne Impellizzeri, Pittsburgh, Pennsylvania

Serves 12 to 16

"I've probably been making this divine recipe for over twenty years. I began making it in New York and have served it at many functions from Florida to South Carolina and now in Pittsburgh. Everywhere I take it, it's a smash hit."

CRUST

1 cup chocolate wafer crumbs

¼ cup (½ stick) butter, melted

FILLING

Two 8-ounce packages cream cheese, softened

¾ cup sugar

3 eggs, at room temperature

1½ teaspoons vanilla extract

5 ounces semisweet chocolate squares, melted and cooled

1 cup plain yogurt

CHOCOLATE GLAZE

3 ounces semisweet chocolate squares

2 tablespoons butter

½ teaspoon vanilla extract

1. Preheat the oven to 300°F.

2. To prepare the crust, combine the wafer crumbs and melted butter in a small bowl; mix well. Press into the bottom of a 9-inch springform pan or a 9-inch deep-dish pie pan.

3. To prepare the filling, combine the cream cheese and sugar in a large bowl. Beat until smooth with a mixer at medium-high speed. Beat in the eggs and vanilla. Stir in melted chocolate and yogurt; mix well. Pour into the prepared crust.

4. Place the dish in the oven. Place a pan of water on the bottom oven rack. Bake for 50 to 60 minutes, until the edges of the cheesecake pull away from the sides of the pan. Do not open the oven door while baking. Cool in the oven with the door open.

5. To prepare the glaze, combine the chocolate, butter, and vanilla in a small saucepan. Place the pan over low heat until the chocolate and butter are melted and the mixture is smooth. Cool slightly and then spread over the cheesecake. Refrigerate until well chilled.

White Chocolate Cheesecake with Raspberry Glaze

Judy Clouse, Golva, North Dakota

*"T*his cheesecake takes a little bit more time and effort, but it is worth it for special occasions. I've served it to our bishop and several times to my siblings and family."

1. Preheat the oven to 350°F. Grease a 9-inch springform pan.

2. To prepare the crust, combine the graham cracker crumbs, sugar, cinnamon, and melted butter in a medium bowl. Using a fork, stir until well blended. Press into the bottom of the prepared pan.

3. To prepare the filling, combine the cream cheese, eggs, sugar, vanilla, and lemon juice in a large bowl. Beat until smooth with a mixer at medium speed. Pour into the crust. Bake for 25 minutes. Remove from the oven and cool for 5 minutes. Maintain the oven temperature.

4. To prepare the topping, combine the sour cream, sugar, vanilla, and white chocolate in a bowl; blend well. Spread over the cheesecake. Bake for 20 to 25 minutes longer, until set. Cool and then refrigerate the cheesecake until well chilled, preferably overnight.

5. To prepare the glaze, combine the raspberries, cornstarch, and sugar in a medium saucepan. Cook over medium heat for 7 to 10 minutes, until the mixture is thick and smooth, stirring constantly. Strain through a fine-mesh sieve, if desired. At serving time, drizzle the glaze over the cheesecake.

CRUST

1½ cups graham cracker crumbs

3 tablespoons sugar

½ teaspoon ground cinnamon

⅓ cup (5⅓ tablespoons) melted butter

FILLING

Two 8-ounce packages cream cheese, softened

2 eggs

¾ cup sugar

2 tablespoons vanilla extract

1 tablespoon lemon juice

TOPPING

2 cups sour cream

¼ cup sugar

2 teaspoons vanilla extract

10 ounces white chocolate, finely chopped

GLAZE

One 12-ounce package frozen unsweetened raspberries

1½ tablespoons cornstarch

½ cup sugar

Carolyn's Morsels

Carolyn Hayes, Elba, New York

Makes 6 dozen cookies

"*T*his is my own cookie that I cloned from a secret recipe. It took me two weeks to perfect it—and mine is better."

2½ cups all-purpose flour

½ teaspoon baking powder

½ teaspoon salt

1 cup (2 sticks) butter, cut into
    tablespoons

1½ cups packed light brown sugar

1 tablespoon vanilla extract

2 eggs, at room temperature

1 cup chopped pecans

One 8-ounce package toffee bits

One 8-ounce package milk chocolate
    chips

One 8-ounce package semisweet
    chocolate chips

1. Preheat the oven to 325°F.

2. Stir together the flour, baking powder, and salt in a large bowl. Cream the butter until light and fluffy with a mixer at medium-high speed. Add the brown sugar and vanilla; mix well.

3. Combine the eggs and 1 teaspoon water in a small bowl; beat with a fork. Add to the creamed mixture; beat well.

4. Add the flour mixture to the creamed mixture and beat at low speed just until combined. Stir in the pecans, toffee bits, and chocolate chips. Chill for 1 hour, or until the dough is firm.

5. Drop the dough by tablespoonfuls onto an ungreased baking sheet. Bake for about 10 minutes, until lightly browned on the edges only. Cool on wire racks.

Healthy Heart Cookies

Anne Crawford, Auburn, Kentucky

Makes 1½ dozen cookies

"I come from a large family in southern Indiana, and the most prevalent health hazard for us is heart disease. So I came up with these healthy cookies. They taste good enough to feel like we're cheating, even when we're not."

1. Preheat the oven to 350°F. Line a baking sheet with parchment paper.

2. Combine the yogurt, brown sugar blend, and buttery spread in a bowl; mix until light and fluffy. Stir in the oats, dried fruit, cinnamon, and pecans.

3. Drop by teaspoonfuls onto the prepared baking sheet. Press together and flatten with a fork for uniform baking. Bake for 10 minutes for a chewy texture or 15 minutes for crisper cookies.

1 cup plain fat-free yogurt

½ cup Splenda brown sugar blend

2 tablespoons Smart Balance buttery spread, not light variety, melted

1½ cups quick-cooking oats

½ cup dried fruit, such as cranberries or blueberries

¼ teaspoon ground cinnamon

¼ cup chopped pecans or almonds

Molasses Spice Drop Cookies

Betty Cochran, West Danville, Vermont

Makes 30 cookies

"*I* tell everyone this is my husband's favorite cookie in the whole wide world, and now it has become the same for my grandchildren and great-grandchildren!"

¾ cup vegetable shortening

1 cup sugar

1 egg

¼ cup molasses

2 cups all-purpose flour

2 teaspoons baking soda

½ teaspoon salt

1 teaspoon ground cinnamon

1 teaspoon ground cloves

1 teaspoon ground ginger

1. Preheat the oven to 375°F. Grease a baking sheet.

2. Combine the shortening, sugar, egg, and molasses in a large bowl. Beat until well blended with a mixer at medium speed.

3. Sift together the remaining ingredients in a separate bowl. Add to the shortening mixture. Beat on low just until blended.

4. Roll the dough into walnut-size balls. Do not flatten. Arrange on the prepared baking sheet. Bake for 9 minutes for soft cookies and 10 minutes for crisper cookies.

Pumpkin Pudding Dip

Christine Dellecave, Scranton, Pennsylvania

Serves 32

"I make this recipe quite a bit for family occasions. I made it once on Thanksgiving Day for the doctors and nurses who were stuck at the hospital where I work and couldn't spend the holiday with their families."

1. Combine the cream cheese, ricotta, pumpkin, sugar, and ground cinnamon in a large bowl.

2. Beat until just blended with a mixer at low speed. Increase the speed to medium-high and beat until fluffy. Cover with plastic wrap and refrigerate until serving time. Serve with whipped topping. Use as a pudding or dip for fruit or shortbread cookies.

One 8-ounce package cream cheese or reduced-fat cream cheese, softened
One 15-ounce container ricotta cheese (may use part-skim)
One 16-ounce can pumpkin purée
2 cups sugar or Splenda
1½ tablespoons ground cinnamon
One 8-ounce container frozen whipped topping, thawed
Fruit
Shortbread cookies

TIPS FROM OUR TEST KITCHEN: This recipe may be halved.

Quick Apple Dumplings

Linda Walker, Smithville, Tennessee

"I have four girls who all live out of town. Every time they call to say they are coming home, they want to know if I am going to make them apple dumplings, they love them so much."

2 medium Granny Smith apples
One 8-count package refrigerated
    crescent roll dough
1/8 teaspoon ground cinnamon
1/2 cup (1 stick) butter or margarine
1 cup sugar
1 cup orange juice
1 teaspoon vanilla extract
1/2 cup chopped pecans, crushed
Ice cream, optional

1. Preheat the oven to 350°F. Grease an 8-inch-square baking dish.

2. Peel and core the apples. Cut each apple into quarters. Unroll and separate the crescent roll dough. Wrap each apple section in one crescent roll. Place in the prepared pan. Sprinkle with the cinnamon.

3. Combine the butter, sugar, and orange juice in a medium saucepan. Bring to a boil, remove from the heat, and stir in the vanilla. Pour over the dumplings. Sprinkle the pecans over the top.

4. Bake for 30 minutes, or until the crust is golden and beginning to bubble and the apples are just tender when pierced with a fork.

5. To serve, place the dumplings on serving plates and spoon some of the syrup from the baking dish over the dumplings. Serve with ice cream, if using.

Grace's Apple Surprise

Grace Lloyd, Oxford, Georgia

"I was in a hurry and didn't want to make a piecrust, so I whipped up this apple dish. It turned out so well and tastes better than pie. My family loves it, so I make it often."

1. Preheat the oven to 350°F.

2. Place the apple slices in an 11×7-inch baking dish.

3. Combine the flour, sugar, baking powder, salt, and egg in a bowl; mix until crumbly using a fork. Sprinkle over the apples.

4. Pour the melted butter over the top and sprinkle with the cinnamon. Bake for 35 to 45 minutes, until the apples are cooked and the top is lightly browned. Serve in glass dessert dishes. Add a scoop of ice cream, if using.

6 medium apples, such as Gala, peeled, if desired, and sliced

1 cup all-purpose flour

1½ cups sugar

1 teaspoon baking powder

¾ teaspoon salt

1 egg

½ cup (1 stick) butter, melted

½ teaspoon ground cinnamon

Ice cream, optional

Fudge Cappuccino Orange Torte

Michelle Gauer, Spicer, Minnesota

Serves 12 to 16

"I have always loved the combination of rich chocolate and orange. I make it on my birthday and treat everyone else to it. I also served it for a women's dessert luncheon at my church and everyone raved about it."

BASE

1 teaspoon instant coffee granules

One 16-ounce package fudge brownie mix

½ cup (1 stick) butter, softened

¼ cup vegetable oil

1 to 2 teaspoons grated orange zest

¼ cup orange juice

2 eggs

4 ounces sweet dark or semisweet baking chocolate, coarsely chopped

FILLING

1 cup sweetened condensed milk

6 ounces sweet dark or semisweet baking chocolate, finely chopped

2 egg yolks, slightly beaten

2 tablespoons orange juice

¾ cup pecan pieces, toasted, if desired, and finely chopped

1. Preheat the oven to 350°F. Grease the bottom only of a 9- or 10-inch springform pan.

2. To prepare the base, combine ¼ cup hot water and the coffee granules in a small bowl; set aside to cool.

3. Combine the brownie mix, butter, oil, orange zest, orange juice, eggs, and the coffee mixture in a large bowl; beat 50 strokes with a spoon. Stir in the chopped chocolate. Spread into the prepared pan.

4. Bake for 35 to 45 minutes, until the center is just set. Do not overbake. Cool completely on a wire rack.

5. To prepare the filling, combine the sweetened condensed milk and the chocolate in a medium saucepan. Cook over low heat, stirring occasionally, until the chocolate is just melted and the mixture is smooth. Remove from the heat.

6. Place the egg yolks in a small bowl and quickly stir in 2 tablespoons of the hot chocolate mixture until well blended. Gradually stir the yolk mixture into the chocolate mixture in the saucepan. Cook over medium heat for 3 minutes, stirring constantly. Remove from the heat; stir in the orange juice and pecans. Refrigerate about 25 minutes, until cool.

Spread the cooled filling mixture over the brownie base. Refrigerate at least 1 hour or until the filling is set.

7. To prepare the topping, combine the heavy cream, confectioners' sugar, cocoa, orange zest, orange juice, and salt in a large bowl. Beat until blended with a mixer at low speed. Increase the speed to high and beat until stiff peaks form.

8. To serve, run a knife around the sides of the springform pan to loosen. Remove the sides of the pan and place the torte on a serving plate. Pipe or spoon the topping mixture evenly over the filling. Garnish with orange slices or mint leaves, if using, or top with a raspberry or strawberry fan and shaved chocolate, if using.

TOPPING

1½ cups heavy cream

¾ cup confectioners' sugar

⅓ cup cocoa powder

1 to 3 teaspoons grated orange zest

2 tablespoons orange juice

⅛ teaspoon salt

Orange slices, optional

Mint leaves, optional

Raspberries or strawberries, optional

Shaved chocolate

GRAND PRIZE WINNER IN AMERICAN PROFILE MAGAZINE'S HOMETOWN GET-TOGETHERS RECIPE CONTEST

Fresh Peach Cobbler

Bette Lou Wolford, Fort Morgan, Colorado

Serves 12

"*I* have taken this recipe to many potlucks, and it is always enjoyed by everyone and the recipe is always requested."

CRUST

2 cups all-purpose flour

1 teaspoon salt

1 cup vegetable shortening

FILLING

¼ cup all-purpose flour

1 cup sugar

¼ teaspoon ground cinnamon

½ teaspoon salt

2½ to 3 pounds fresh peaches, peeled, pitted, and sliced

½ cup peach preserves

1 tablespoon lemon juice

¼ cup (½ stick) butter

1 egg, well beaten

1. Preheat the oven to 425°F. Grease a 13×9-inch cake pan.

2. To prepare the crust, combine the flour and salt in a large mixing bowl. Using a pastry blender, cut in the shortening until the mixture resembles coarse crumbs. Mix in ½ cup water until the dough forms a soft ball. Place between two sheets of parchment or wax paper and roll to 9 x 13 inches. Set aside.

3. To prepare the filling, combine the flour, sugar, cinnamon, and salt in a large bowl. Add the peaches, preserves, and ⅓ cup water; mix well. Pour into the prepared pan. Sprinkle with the lemon juice and dot with the butter. Top with the crust. Lightly brush the top of the crust with the beaten egg.

4. Bake for 10 minutes. Reduce the oven temperature to 350°F. Bake for 30 to 45 minutes longer, until the crust is browned.

TIPS FROM OUR TEST KITCHEN: For cherry cobbler, use 5 to 6 cups pitted cherries and additional sugar to taste. Omit the preserves and cinnamon and add 1 teaspoon almond extract.

Peanut Butter Cup Dessert

Elizabeth Yoder, Berne, Indiana

Serves 12 to 16

"I like to take this recipe to family get-togethers. There's never any left to take home!"

1. Preheat the oven to 350°F. Grease a 13×9-inch baking pan.

2. To prepare the bottom layer, combine the butter, granulated sugar, egg, and vanilla in a large mixing bowl. Cream the mixture until fluffy with a mixer at medium-high speed. Reduce the heat to low and add the flour, cocoa, baking soda, and salt. Beat just until blended. Press into the prepared pan.

3. Bake for 10 minutes. Cool completely.

4. To prepare the middle layer, combine the cream cheese, peanut butter, and confectioners' sugar in a medium bowl. Beat until well blended with a mixer at medium speed. Add the whipped topping and mix until smooth and creamy. Spread over the cooled bottom layer.

5. To prepare the top layer, spread the whipped topping over the middle layer. Sprinkle the chopped peanut butter cups on top. Cover and refrigerate until serving time.

BOTTOM LAYER

½ cup (1 stick) butter or margarine, softened

1 cup granulated sugar

1 egg

1 teaspoon vanilla extract

1¼ cups all-purpose flour

½ cup cocoa powder

¾ teaspoon baking soda

¼ teaspoon salt

MIDDLE LAYER

One 8-ounce package cream cheese, softened

¾ cup creamy peanut butter

1 cup confectioners' sugar

One 8-ounce container frozen whipped topping, thawed

TOP LAYER

One 8-ounce container frozen whipped topping, thawed

10 peanut butter cups, coarsely chopped

Walnut Dainties

Betty Maithonis, Canyon Country, California

Serves 16

"I have made this recipe for fifty years, and every time I make it, I'm asked for the recipe."

¾ cup butter, softened (no substitutes)
1½ cups packed light brown sugar
1 egg
1 teaspoon vanilla extract
1½ cups all-purpose flour
1 teaspoon baking powder
⅛ teaspoon salt
1 cup finely chopped walnuts
Whipped cream, optional

1. Preheat the oven to 350°F. Grease an 8-inch-square baking pan.

2. Cream the butter and brown sugar with a mixer at medium speed. Add the egg and vanilla; mix well.

3. Reduce the speed to low and mix in the flour, baking powder, salt, and walnuts. Spread the batter in the prepared pan.

4. Bake for 30 to 40 minutes, until browned. Cool completely. Serve with whipped cream, if using.

Ultimate Apple Pie

Barbara Schindler, Napoleon, Ohio

Serves 6 to 8

"*T*his pie is asked for at all of our family get-togethers. I usually bake two pies—but ten would not be enough!"

1. To prepare the crust, combine the flour, Cheddar, and salt in a bowl. Using a pastry blender, cut in the shortening until the mixture resembles coarse crumbs. Add the vanilla and 4 or 5 tablespoons ice water. Blend until the mixture forms a ball.

2. Divide the dough into two sections, one twice as large as the other. Roll the larger portion on a floured board or between two pieces of wax paper to form the bottom crust. Fit into a 9-inch deep-dish pie plate, letting the excess dough hang over the sides.

3. Preheat the oven to 400°F.

4. To prepare the filling, combine the tapioca, sugar, cinnamon, nutmeg, and salt in a large bowl. Add the apples and orange zest; mix well. Spoon the filling into the prepared crust. Roll out the remaining dough. Place over the apple mixture, pinching the crusts together. Cut slits in the top.

5. To prepare the glaze, combine the egg yolk and milk in a small bowl. Brush lightly over the crust. Sprinkle with the sugar, if using.

6. Cover the pie lightly with foil. Bake for 30 to 45 minutes, until the apples are almost tender when

CRUST

2 cups all-purpose flour

1 cup shredded Cheddar

¼ teaspoon salt

⅔ cup vegetable shortening

1 teaspoon vanilla extract

FILLING

2 tablespoons quick-cooking tapioca

¾ cup sugar

1 teaspoon ground cinnamon

¼ teaspoon nutmeg

¼ teaspoon salt

7 or 8 baking apples, such as Gala, peeled, cored, and sliced

2 teaspoons grated orange zest

GLAZE

1 egg yolk

2 tablespoons milk

1 teaspoon sugar, optional

continued

TOPPING

1 cup chopped dates

1 cup chopped toasted walnuts

1 cup maple syrup

pierced through the crust with a fork. Remove the foil and bake for 10 to 15 minutes longer, until the crust is browned.

7. To prepare the topping, combine the dates, walnuts, and maple syrup. Spoon over the entire pie or on top of individual servings.

Buttermilk Pie

Tommie Haferkamp, Gatesville, Texas

Serves 6 to 8

"*M*y mother was born in 1900 and was one of twelve children, seven of whom were girls. Grandma Powell, her mother, was a good cook, as were all the daughters. They were famous for their Buttermilk Pie."

1. Preheat the oven to 325°F.

2. Combine the sugar, flour, and salt in a bowl; mix well. Blend in the eggs. Add the butter, buttermilk, and vanilla; mix well. Pour the mixture into the piecrust.

3. Bake for 60 to 65 minutes, until a knife inserted near the center comes out clean. The center may still look wet.

1½ cups sugar

3 tablespoons all-purpose flour

⅛ teaspoon salt

4 eggs, well beaten

½ cup (1 stick) butter, melted

1 cup buttermilk

1 teaspoon vanilla extract

1 unbaked 9-inch deep-dish piecrust

Coconut Cream Cheese Pies

Carolyn Lawson, Kannapolis, North Carolina

Serves 12 to 16

"I've used this recipe for a Sunday gathering and it was very well liked. It's good for suppers, family reunions, and many other occasions."

Two 8-ounce packages cream cheese,
  softened
1½ cups sugar
2 tablespoons all-purpose flour
2 eggs
8 ounces sour cream
2 teaspoons lemon juice
One 6-ounce bag frozen coconut, thawed
2 graham cracker piecrusts

1. Preheat the oven to 325°F.

2. Combine the cream cheese, sugar, and flour in a bowl. Beat until smooth with a mixer at medium-high speed. Add the eggs, one at a time, and beat until well blended. Add the sour cream, lemon juice, and all but ¼ cup of the coconut, beating well after each addition.

3. Pour into the piecrusts and bake for 35 to 45 minutes, until set. Refrigerate for 3 hours or until completely cooled. Sprinkle the remaining ¼ cup coconut on top of the pies. Refrigerate until ready to serve.

Cran-Raspberry Pie

Mary Ann Kauchak, Woodbridge, Virginia

Serves 6 to 8

"*S*everal years ago, I created this pie. It is now a family favorite for Christmas and a must when company comes. It is tart, yet sweet, and makes a colorful addition to any table. My mom's streusel topping gives this pie a homemade touch."

1. Preheat the oven to 425°F.

2. To prepare the filling, spoon the cranberry sauce into a large bowl. Break up the sauce with a spoon. Stir in the raspberries and tapioca. Let the mixture stand for 15 minutes. Pour the filling into the piecrust.

3. To prepare the topping, combine the flour, sugar, and butter in a small bowl. Mix with a fork until crumbly. Sprinkle the topping evenly over the fruit.

4. Bake for 30 minutes, or until brown and bubbly.

FILLING

Two 16-ounce cans whole-berry cranberry sauce

One 12-ounce bag frozen unsweetened raspberries, thawed

2 tablespoons quick-cooking tapioca

One 9-inch unbaked piecrust

STREUSEL TOPPING

½ cup all-purpose flour

¼ cup sugar

¼ cup (½ stick) cold butter or margarine

Fresh Fruit Pies

Carole VanCleave, Concord, North Carolina

Serves 12 to 16

"As my time has always been limited, I like easy-to-make dishes. This recipe has always served me well at holiday dinners, family gatherings, and church functions."

1 cup heavy cream
One 8-ounce package cream cheese, softened
Juice of 1 medium lemon (2 tablespoons)
1 cup sugar
2 graham cracker piecrusts
2½ cups sliced fresh strawberries
2 cups sliced fresh peaches

1. Combine the cream, cream cheese, lemon juice, and sugar in a large bowl. Beat until smooth with a mixer at medium-high speed. Spread half of the mixture in the bottom of each piecrust. Refrigerate for 2 hours, or until set.

2. Remove the pies from the refrigerator and arrange the fruit on top of each. Return to the refrigerator overnight.

Easy Arizona Lemon Pie

June Laughlin, Lady Lake, Florida

"Yummy!"

1. Preheat the oven to 350°F.
2. Cut up the lemon and place in a blender. Add the eggs, sugar, and butter. Blend on high for 3 minutes. Pour the mixture into the piecrust.
3. Place a baking sheet on an oven rack. Place the piecrust on the baking sheet. Bake for 35 to 40 minutes, until set.

1 large Meyer lemon or 1 organic lemon, peel left on
4 eggs
1½ cups sugar
½ cup (1 stick) butter, softened
1 unbaked 9-inch piecrust

TIPS FROM OUR TEST KITCHEN: This is the easiest pie you'll ever make. It explodes with great lemon flavor.

Old-Fashioned Sweet Potato Pies for a Crowd

Debra Davis, Texarkana, Arkansas

Serves 24

"*I* bake these pies for church suppers and family get-togethers. They never stay around for long. Someone told me that they have just the right sweetness. Eat this pie with a passion—um, um good."

Four 9-inch unbaked frozen piecrusts
2 pounds sweet potatoes, peeled and cooked
2 cups sugar
1½ cups (3 sticks) butter, softened
2 teaspoons ground nutmeg
1 teaspoon ground cinnamon
2 teaspoons vanilla extract
1 cup evaporated milk
3 medium egg yolks

1. Preheat the oven to 400°F.

2. Thaw the piecrusts for 15 minutes. Prick the bottom and sides and bake for 7 minutes, or until slightly browned. Remove from the oven and reduce the oven temperature to 325°F.

3. Place the sweet potatoes in a large bowl. Beat until well mashed with a mixer at medium-high speed. Add the sugar, butter, nutmeg, cinnamon, and vanilla to the potatoes alternately with the evaporated milk. Beat until smooth.

4. Add the egg yolks and beat until incorporated. Pour the filling into the piecrusts. Bake for 40 to 50 minutes, until the pies are firm. Cover the crusts with foil if they begin to brown too much.

TIPS FROM OUR TEST KITCHEN: This recipe may be halved easily.

Cheesy Peachy Pie

Dana Andrews, Sault St. Marie, Michigan

Serves 6 to 8

*"T*he place where I work is known for the tasty treats we have at our potlucks. We have a potluck once a month, and it's a fun and appetizing get-together. Everyone's favorite dish is always my Cheesy Peachy Pie."

1. Preheat the oven to 425°F.

2. To prepare the crust, combine the flour and salt in a large bowl. Cut in the shortening and butter until the mixture has the texture of peas. Drain the peaches and reserve the syrup. Sprinkle 6 to 7 tablespoons of the syrup over the mixture and stir with a fork until the dough holds together. Reserve the remaining syrup for Cheesecake Filling.

3. Roll out half of the dough on a floured surface to a circle 1½ inches larger than an inverted 9-inch pie plate. Fit the dough into the plate. Roll out the remaining dough.

4. To prepare the peach filling, combine the peaches, sugar, cornstarch, corn syrup, pumpkin pie spice, and vanilla in a large bowl; mix well. Pour into the pie plate and dot with the butter.

5. To prepare the cheesecake filling, combine the cream cheese and sour cream in a small bowl; mix until smooth. Combine the eggs, sugar, lemon juice, and 2 tablespoons peach syrup in a small saucepan. Cook over medium heat for 4 minutes, or until thick, whisking constantly. Stir in the cream cheese mixture and whisk until smooth. Pour on top of the peach filling.

CRUST

2 cups all-purpose flour

1 teaspoon salt

⅔ cup vegetable shortening

2 tablespoons butter

One 15-ounce can sliced peaches, packed in heavy syrup

PEACH FILLING

½ cup sugar

3 tablespoons cornstarch

2 tablespoons light corn syrup

2 teaspoons pumpkin pie spice

2 teaspoons vanilla extract

1 tablespoon butter

CHEESECAKE FILLING

One 3-ounce package cream cheese, softened

continued

½ **cup sour cream**

2 eggs

⅓ **cup sugar**

1 tablespoon lemon juice

6. Cover the top of the pie with the remaining crust. Make slits in the top crust. Bake for 10 minutes. Reduce the oven temperature to 350°F. Bake for 35 minutes, or until golden brown.

List of Contributors

Ableidinger, Dorothea *New Prague, Minnesota*

Adams, Janice *Jefferson, Wisconsin*

Andrews, Dana *Sault St. Marie, Michigan*

Arnold, Elaine *Altus, Oklahoma*

Bagley, Betty *Athens, Tennessee*

Baumgartner, Elda *Rossiter, Pennsylvania*

Bazor, Sylvia *Covington, Tennessee*

Berry, Margee *Trout Lake, Washington*

Bertaccini, Albert & Julia *Old Forge, Pennsylvania*

Bier, Linda *Hannibal, Missouri*

Biggs, Phyllis *Dobson, North Carolina*

Bilke, Mary *Eagle River, Wisconsin*

Bonsall, Judith *Hillsdale, Michigan*

Bornemann, Stacey *Center, North Dakota*

Bosch, Ethan *Clarion, Pennsylvania*

Boutin, Cheryl *Willcox, Arizona*

Bradford, Joe *Sea Island, Georgia*

Bradley, Denise *Bowling Green, Kentucky*

Breedlove, Virginia *Wharton, Texas*

Brintle, Sue *Mount Airy, North Carolina*

Brody, Josephine *Donora, Pennsylvania*

Brown, Pauline *Chinquapin, North Carolina*

Bruere, Carole *Albuquerque, New Mexico*

Bullen, Mary *Gibsonia, Pennsylvania*

Burkett, Stephanie *Chico, California*

Campanelli, Maria *New Bern, North Carolina*

Carlson, Lois *Palisade, Minnesota*

Carlsten, Libby *Los Alamos, New Mexico*

Carrion, Jill *St. Cloud, Florida*

Carter, Carlene *Lincoln, Illinois*

Chapman, Barbara *Casper, Wyoming*

Chitwood, Helen *McKinleyville, California*

Christofferson, Jan *Eagle River, Wisconsin*

Clonch, Dorothy *Hopkinsville, Kentucky*

Clouse, Judy *Golva, North Dakota*

Cochran, Betty *West Danville, Vermont*

Cooper, Janice *Argos, Indiana*

Coverston, Dorothy *Coeur d'Alene, Idaho*

Crawford, Anne *Auburn, Kentucky*

Crumpton, Sheryl *Lindale, Texas*

Crunk, Karen *Lorena, Texas*

Cumpton, Elsie *Worthington, Kentucky*

Davis, Debra *Texarkana, Arkansas*

Dellecave, Christine *Scranton, Pennsylvania*

Dicharo, Kathy *Bryan, Texas*

Donath, Liz *Philadelphia, Missouri*

DuBovy, Millie   *Lady Lake, Florida*

Duhon, Lillie   *Port Neches, Texas*

Fetter, Elaine   *Rittman, Ohio*

Fiore, Lea   *Marble, North Carolina*

Froehlich, Eleanor   *Rochester Hills, Michigan*

Galbraith, Edgar D.   *Jacksonville, North Carolina*

Gauer, Michelle   *Spicer, Minnesota*

Gawne, Robert   *Waymart, Pennsylvania*

Geary, JoAnn   *Whispering Pines, North Carolina*

Gilliand, Cindy   *Augusta, Kansas*

Goddard, Audie   *Glen Burnie, Maryland*

Gorecki, Jan   *Montague, Michigan*

Gray, Page   *Duncan, Oklahoma*

Greenly, Eleanor   *Levittown, Pennsylvania*

Guiffre, Barbara   *Herkimer, New York*

Haferkamp, Tommie   *Gatesville, Texas*

Hammond, Kimberly   *Kingwood, Texas*

Hauck, Clara   *Richardton, North Dakota*

Hayes, Carolyn   *Elba, New York*

Helfrich, Eric   *Wilkes-Barre, Pennsylvania*

Henderson, Rachel   *The Villages, Florida*

Hutchins, Jeannie   *Newport, Washington*

Impellizzeri, Roseanne   *Pittsburgh, Pennsylvania*

Jacobson, Beth   *Green Spring, West Virginia*

Jaskolka, Mary   *Hot Springs, Arkansas*

Jenkins, Mary Ann   *Gridley, California*

Jordan, Sandra   *Graham, North Carolina*

Joyner, Eleanor   *Loveland, Colorado*

Julow, Lillian   *Gainesville, Florida*

Kaiser, Tammi   *Glenview, Illinois*

Kauchak, Mary Ann   *Woodbridge, Virginia*

Keudell, Kathy   *Columbia City, Oregon*

Key, Betty   *Gardendale, Alabama*

Kivett, Beverly   *Madras, Oregon*

Koivisto, Laverne   *Ashtabula, Ohio*

Kruse, Trisha   *Eagle, Idaho*

Lakin, Josie   *Pikeville, Kentucky*

Langenfeld, Ann   *Burns, Oregon*

Lasseter, Mrs. Norvell   *Waco, Texas*

Laughlin, June   *Lady Lake, Florida*

Lawon, Carolyn   *Kannapolis, North Carolina*

Lawshe, Patricia   *Kalispell, Montana*

Lehmann, Judy   *Ida Grove, Iowa*

Lewis, Vina   *Fortuna, California*

Lloyd, Grace   *Oxford, Georgia*

Lockwood, Shirley   *Constantine, Michigan*

Logan, Verma   *Ardmore, Oklahoma*

Lowe, Christina   *Whittier, California*

Maithonis, Betty   *Canyon Country, California*

Martin, Bonita   *Danville, Pennsylvania*

Massaro, Anthony G.   *Monroeville, Pennsylvania*

Mattox, Bonnie   *Albuquerque, New Mexico*

Mayland, Jan   *Shepherd, Montana*

Maynes, Esmeralda   *Clayton, New Mexico*

McClelland, Carol Ann   *Somers, Connecticut*

McCormick, Jennifer Langworthy   *Irvine, Kentucky*

McCrory, Diane   *Trinity, Texas*

McGinty, Francine   *Spokane, Washington*

Merriman, Malanna   *Oakland City, Indiana*

Mersereau, Marilee   *Manteno, Illinois*

Mileti, Elvira   *Columbia City, Oregon*

Morgan, Robbie   *Myrtle Point, Oregon*

Mrachek, Connie   *Charles City, Iowa*

Murphy, Ashley   *Hastings, Nebraska*

Myers, Karla   *Cedar Rapids, Iowa*

Nemitz, Diane   *Ludington, Michigan*

Nickel, Wendy   *Kiester, Minnesota*

Novak, Kathryn   *Northville, Michigan*

Onuffer, Dawn   *Crestview, Florida*

Ostergaard, Colleen   *Kaysville, Utah*

Ozmina, Marianne   *Warrior Run, Pennsylvania*

Paszko, Debra   *Effort, Pennsylvania*

Petrosky, Loretta   *Lower Burrell, Pennsylvania*

Piazza, Nancy   *Lucerne, California*

Pierce, Drichelle   *Albuquerque, New Mexico*

Pineda, Mike   *Carlsbad, New Mexico*

Richards, Donna   *Tucson, Arizona*

Roberts, Donna   *Shumway, Illinois*

Rowland, Mrs. Clay   *Marion, Virginia*

Russell, Ellen   *LeMars, Iowa*

Scaringi, M. Vicianna   *Verona, Pennsylvania*

Schindler, Barbara   *Napoleon, Ohio*

Schwartz, Delilah E.   *Berne, Indiana*

Shank, Pamela   *Parkersburg, West Virginia*

Shires, Linda   *Caldwell, West Virginia*

Smith, Vickie   *Warsaw, Missouri*

Snyder, Carol   *Sumner, Iowa*

Stephens, Waneta   *Mount Pulaski, Illinois*

Stevens, Gloria   *Kingsville, Ohio*

Stieber, Elaine   *Norwalk, Ohio*

Sweeney, Dan   *Green River, Wyoming*

Taylor, Wanda   *Gould, Oklahoma*

Thureen, Louise   *Two Harbors, Minnesota*

Tomme, Pat   *Brownwood, Texas*

Turner, Connie   *Crossville, Tennessee*

Upchurch, Tammy   *Monticello, Kentucky*

Van Cleave, Carole   *Concord, North Carolina*

Walker, Linda   *Smithville, Tennessee*

Washam, Chicky   *Odessa, Missouri*

Webster, Julia   *Cadiz, Kentucky*

Welch, Jamie   *Tilghman, Maryland*

Welch, Willis J.   *Shelbyville, Tennessee*

Wieberg, Shirley   *Penn Valley, California*

Wilder, Vicki   *Englewood, Florida*

Wilhelmsen, Melanie Myrtle   *Ogden, Utah*

Wolford, Bette Lou   *Fort Morgan, Colorado*

Woods, Jane   *Fort Worth, Texas*

Worthington, Michelle   *Winchester, Kentucky*

Wright, Judith Collier   *Lake Almanor, California*

Wydra, Linda   *Wapwallopen, Pennsylvania*

Yoder, Elizabeth   *Berne, Indiana*

Zant, Patsy   *Lamesa, Texas*

Index